Uneasy Chairs

Errata

Apologies from the Editor and Publisher

We have tried to maintain the differences in style throughout the volume. Unfortunately we have managed to incorporate several typographical errors which were not intended by the authors.

Corrections:

Page iii   Line 18: *Robbins Report.* Footnote: *pseudonym*

Page 31   Line 4 *responded* rather than responses

Page 41   Line 10: *seen* rather than been

Page 63   Line 1: *an* rather than a

Page 64   Line 1: *was* rather than were

Page 71   Title should read: *Constructive* Tension

Page 78   Line 9 should read: 'of which current *research* is but a part'

Page 79   Line 20-21 should read: 'running with their *own agendas...*'

Page 80   Line 21: *continued* rather than continue

Uneasy Chairs:

life as a professor

Edited by
Jeffrey Richards

Innovation in
Higher Education Series

Unit for Innovation
in Higher Education
School of Independent Studies
Lonsdale College
Lancaster University
Lancaster LAI 4YN

First published in 1997 by the Unit for
Innovation in Higher Education, School of
Independent Studies, Lonsdale College
Lancaster University, Lancaster LA1 4YN

ISBN 1-86220-042-4

PRINTED ON
RECYCLED PAPER

Cover design by Rowland & Hird, Lancaster
Printed in Great Britain by
Ampersand Print Management Limited
Preston, Lancashire

Preface by the Series Editor

By the year 2000 Britain will have transformed its elite universities and colleges into a system of mass higher education. With expansion of student numbers and broadening of access it has become increasingly important to understand life at today's universities and colleges, too frequently presented in outdated stereotypes.

So, we are looking for first-hand accounts of experience at the modern university or college of traditional and modern teaching and assessment methods. We would be interested in accounts of all aspects of these institutions such as issues of race, class, age or gender; success and failure; finance; social life and the problems faced by those combining study with jobs and family responsibilities. Appreciation of these issues is crucial not only for students wishing to make the most of their higher education but also for the success of tutors and other staff in providing it.

If you are already – or about to be – involved in higher education in any way, as a student, professor, lecturer, research worker or other staff, we would like to invite you to consider describing and analysing your experience of today's higher education for publication in this series.

John Wakeford

Acknowledgements

We would like to thank *The Times Higher Education Supplement* for their generous and collaborative support. Through their endorsement and support of the IHE Series, we are able to further develop the contributions we are making towards greater understanding of, and improvements to, modern university life.

In particular, we are grateful to Ms Michelle Blore, Marketing Director of *The Times Higher*, for her support of the Series and for her recognition of the significance of these developments.

Sue Weldon
Publications Editor

John Wakeford conceived the idea for this book and passed it on to me for development and execution. Linda Cook transferred the individual contributions to disk and Sue Weldon oversaw production. I am grateful to all of them. But I owe a particular debt of gratitude to the contributors who took time out of very busy schedules to set down their ideas on various aspects of professorial life.

Jeffrey Richards
Editor

Contents

Contributors

John Clayton is Chairman of the Department of Religion and Director of the Graduate Division of Religious and Theological Studies in Boston University. He was formerly Professor of Religious Studies at Lancaster University. He is a Texan.

David Craig is Emeritus Professor of Creative Writing at Lancaster University. He is a noted poet and writer.

Johanna Laybourn-Parry is Professor of Environmental Biology at Nottingham University and previously held a chair at La Trobe University, Melbourne, Australia.

Denis McCaldin is Professor of Performance Studies in Music at Lancaster University. A conductor and musicologist, he is also Director of the Haydn Society of Great Britain.

Ray Macdonald is Professor of Environmental Sciences at Lancaster University. He is a vulcanologist.

Michael Newby is Joslyn Owen Professor of Education and Dean of Arts and Education at Plymouth University.

Trevor Page holds the Cookson Group Chair of Engineering Materials at the University of Newcastle-upon-Tyne.

Jeffrey Richards is Professor of Cultural History at Lancaster University and Chairman of the Cultural Research Institute.

Austin Woolrych is Emeritus Professor of History at Lancaster University. He is a Fellow of the British Academy.

James Wright is Vice-Chancellor of the University of Newcastle-upon-Tyne. He was formerly Professorial Fellow at St Catherine's College, Cambridge. He is a classicist.

Introduction

In his influential and illuminating <u>Red Brick University</u>, first published in 1943, Bruce Truscot defined the job of a professor:

> The life of a well-established, middle-aged professor in the Arts faculty of a modern university can, if he likes to make it so, be one of the softest jobs to be found on the earth's surface. He may live .. fifty miles from his work, and come in for only two or three days a week ... it would probably be no exaggeration to say that ... he need do no more than ten hours' work a week for from twenty-six to twenty-eight weeks in the year.

He went on to outline a typical term-time day in the life of Professor Deadwood:

> He has a leisurely breakfast at half-past eight, followed by pipe and paper; reaches the University between ten and half-past; reads his letters and perhaps writes one; saunters into the Common Room for a cup of coffee; calls on a colleague, or the Bursar, or the Clerk to the Senate; returns to his room, glances through the latest issue of a learned review, has a few words with a pupil - and lo, it's lunchtime. After lunch in the refectory, followed by a chat about the day's news in the Common Room, he gives a lecture at half-past two, and immediately afterwards hurries home lest he should be late for tea. After tea comes the day's exercise and after dinner he spends a couple of hours with a new book on his special subject (or a book from the circulating library on something else), after which, the paper again,

a nightcap and bed at eleven, after a somewhat tiring but thoroughly well-spent day![1]

If this was ever true, it has long ceased to be. Professors are now overwhelmed with work, not just academic but administrative. The burdens are so great and so time-consuming that a number of eminent professors in a variety of disciplines whom I approached to participate in this little venture were, despite their attraction to the project, simply unable to find the time to put their thoughts on paper.

The work of professors seems to have grown in proportion to the expansion of the universities. Truscot was writing when there was only a handful of universities; the Ancient Universities, dating back to the Middle Ages (Oxford, Cambridge, Glasgow, Edinburgh, St Andrew's, etc) and the 'civic' or 'red brick' universities (Manchester, Liverpool, Birmingham, Leeds, Sheffield, Bristol, etc), mainly dating from the first quarter of the 20th century. These were joined, in the wake of the Robbins Reports in the 1960s, by the 'plateglass' or 'new universities' (Lancaster, York, Sussex, Warwick, Kent, Stirling, East Anglia, etc), mainly built on greenfield sites outside old county or cathedral towns. These

---

[1] Bruce Truscot, Red Brick University, Hardmondsworth: Pelican, 1951, pp 99-100, 341-2. The identity of Bruce Truscot was a closely guarded secret. It was only after his death that it became widely known that Bruce Truscot was the pseudonum of Edgar Allison Peers (1891-1952), Gilmour Professor of Spanish at Liverpool University from 1922 to 1952. He coined the term 'Red Brick University' in his books Red Brick University (1943) and These Vital Days (1945). The two books were combined in a revised version, Red Brick University, published by Pelican in 1951. Peers' autobiography Redbrick University Revisited, edited by Ann L Mackenzie and Adrian R Allan, was published by Liverpool University Press in 1996.

have been joined in the 1990s, in the shadow of the Dearing Report, by the 'polyversities' or 'new universities' as the distinction between universities and polytechnics has been abolished. This more than doubled the number of universities at a stroke. There are now more than a hundred in Britain, each with its full complement of professors. Few of them would recognise the lifestyle of Professor Deadwood.

However, the basic role of the professor remains what it was when in the middle of the 19th century John Henry Newman defined the idea of a university.[2] It was a definition which Truscot endorsed in the 1940s and which Lord Annan was still articulating in the 1970s, when he wrote:

> There is really no mystery about the roles of the university. For the past century there has been no dispute about its two main functions. It exists first to promote through reflection and research the life of the mind: second to transmit high culture to each generation. Whatever is thought to be intellectually important and of concern to society it teaches to new students.[3]

In short, the functions of the university are research (the advancement of knowledge) and teaching (the dissemination of knowledge). To do the former involves the professor in conducting primary research, writing books and papers, attending and speaking at and organising conferences, refereeing and reviewing books and articles, serving on the editorial boards of journals, editing scholarly series, delivering

---

[2] John Henry Newman, The Idea of a University, New York: Chelsea House, 1983 reprint.
[3] M D Stephens and G W Roderick eds, Universities for a Changing World, Newton Abbot: David and Charles, 1975, p 19.

lectures to outside bodies and organisations, and generally keeping up with the work in one's field. Teaching at the undergraduate and postgraduate level involves preparing and delivering courses of lectures, small group teaching, setting and marking essays and exercises of various kinds, setting, marking and supervising examinations, writing references, supervising dissertations and generally advising students at all levels on their work.

These two full-time jobs have been joined by a third, which was always there but has been becoming more and more prominent - management. Truscot recognised it in 1943:

> Another - an unremunerative - type of work with which the professor occupies his time is university administration and politics. As has been said, it is an excellent thing that a university should be controlled and organised to the extent that it is by the Senate and the Faculties, and this should mean that, during term, a part of the working week of each of their members is devoted either to the normal meetings or to such special duties as attendance at committees for filling Chairs, library committees, departmental meetings, and so on. But there are two abuses of the system. First, committees of Senates and Faculty Boards are as a rule too numerous, too large and too frequent in their meetings. Secondly, the well-known tendency to overwork the willing horse is nowhere more observable than here. The few people who are clearly fitted for committee work (and sometimes no less clearly unfitted for the more essential activities of university life) are elected to committee after committee, until for half their time they are serving tables, their term-life is spent between lecture-room and

committee-room, and they come home at night unfit for anything but relaxation.[4]

This can make the life of the committee-man professor seem to the outside world to be totally boring. Humphrey Carpenter hints at this in his biography of Professor J R R Tolkien when he writes that in 1925 Tolkien became Professor of Anglo-Saxon at Oxford 'and after this, you might say, nothing else really happened'.[5] Tolkien was Rawlinson and Bosworth Professor of Anglo-Saxon for twenty years and then Merton Professor of English Language and Literature from 1945 until his retirement in 1959. His life consisted of 'domestic routine, teaching, preparation for teaching, correspondence, an occasional evening with friends', interspersed with faculty meetings, examiners' meetings, college meetings.[6] But this was merely the outside scaffolding. There was a rich and fecund inner life, a life of the mind continually at work, which resulted eventually in the production of one of the 20th century's great works of imaginative literature, The Lord of the Rings, the fruit of a lifetime's immersion in the study of myth and language. Not every professor is mentally composing a great work of fiction, but many are constantly mulling over the central problems and themes and debates of their subjects and seeking solutions, explanations and interpretations which they will eventually embody in books and papers, some of which will decisively change the way in which their subject is understood.

Increasingly, however, there are some professors who are mere managers and for whom the life of the imagination

---

[4] Truscot, Red Brick University, p 103.
[5] Humphrey Carpenter, J R R Tolkien, London: Unwin, 1978, p 118.
[6] Carpenter, Tolkien, p 127.

consists of drawing up agendas and compiling minutes. The caricatured business image of the 'good meeting', whole and contained unto itself, is inexorably creeping into university life. The world is progressively scaled down from the universe of thought and reading, research and speculation, the imaginative inner life shrivels, and there is just the scaffolding, the 'everyday affair', as Kipling put it, 'of business, meals and clothing' plus meetings. This is in part the consequence of profound changes in the universities, in particular the introduction of the principle of accountability. It is only right that as recipients of public money, universities should be accountable. Outside assessment is perfectly right and proper. But it has become a non-stop, year-round, twenty-four hours a day business. Academics in general and professors in particular are drowning in an alphabet soup of investigatory procedures. The Research Assessment Exercise (RAE) and the Teaching Quality Audit (TQA) are only the twin peaks of a mountain of paperwork that is being demanded - mission statements, self-assessment, staff appraisals, course rationales, student questionnaires, budget plans, etc. etc. No sooner has one of these exercises ended than another is launched in an unending Kafkaesque bureaucratic nightmare. Some professors have been taken over completely by this work. A new tier of permanent 'senior management' has been introduced, for whom teaching and research have become distant memories.

This has all taken place against a background of increasing financial stringency as year on year cuts in University funding coupled with an expanded student intake has produced a situation of increasing economic hardship, which has led the Committee of Vice-Chancellors and Principals (CVCP) to predict that all universities will be bankrupt by the year 2005. This squeeze on funding has led to departmental closures, the axing of posts, academics forced into early retirement, and a vastly increased workload for those who are left, professors included. Some professors are now appointed to be fund-raisers: others can maintain their chairs only if they raise outside cash to pay themselves.

Academic salaries, including those of professors, have fallen way below those of comparable professionals. Despite this and despite the continuing myths of the 'absent-minded professor', the ivory tower and the 'long holidays', professors still apparently maintain status. The distinguished journalist Peter Hennessy recognised this when he was appointed Professor of Contemporary History at Queen Mary and Westfield College, London. He writes:

> Even in post-Thatcher Britain, money on its own is nowhere. Status is King. Appreciating this intellectually is one thing. Experiencing it oneself is quite another. Only when I became a professor four years ago did the potency of the British status obsession strike me with its full force. The shock was intensified as I had not expected it. Because for years I had thought the English (in contrast to the Scots and Welsh) rather disdained the professional version of status, treating the scholarly calling as some tweedy, rather idle irrelevance ... But the title of professor - and in History to boot - promoted me to a different league. I was definitely poorer, yet infinitely more respectable. It wasn't just the television interviewers ...that reflected this status jump. Civil Service permanent secretaries even began to defer.[7]

Professor Hennessy's media appearances raise the whole question of how professors should profess their subjects in the wider world. There remains a worrying and defensive

---

[7] The Independent, 24 October 1996.

intellectual snobbery in some areas of academe directed towards those professors who seek newspapers, radio and television to communicate their theories, ideas and research to a wider public. A J P Taylor failed to become Regius Professor of History at Oxford in 1957 in part because of his involvement in popular journalism which earned him the scorn of Oxford dons. But such scorn is an attitude exclusive to Britain. In France and Italy it is not at all unusual for leading intellectuals to use all the mass media to communicate with the public. Journalism is after all another form of communication and popularisation like lecturing. There have always been 'telly dons'. Professor Cyril Joad and Professor Sir Mortimer Wheeler are notable examples from an earlier generation, popularising philosophy and archaeology respectively through the mass media. There are several notable current examples of professors who are adept at professing their subjects in the media: Professors Steve Jones, Lewis Wolpert and Colin Blakemore on science, Professors Anthony King, Peter Hennessy and Vernon Bogdanor on the constitution, Professors Lisa Jardine, Christopher Frayling and Marina Warner on culture. A few, on the other hand, become 'rentaquote' experts and encourage a cult of personality which does no favours to the profession or to serious and thoughtful communication.

At the other end of the spectrum, there are too many academics who far from communicating with the public have retreated into an exclusive mandarin language of the higher gobbledegook merely to impress each other. This leaves them in considerable danger of disappearing up their own signifying constructs. Whatever else they may be, academics should never become an isolated, inbred, incestuous coven communicating only with each other. As Umberto Eco, Professor of Semiotics at Bologna University, said: 'Accessibility is a moral duty for academics'. He demonstrated this belief by writing best-selling novels as well as regular newspaper columns alongside his academic monographs.

There are now more professors than ever before in British universities. But the general picture of the professoriate in the 1990s is a mixture of continuity and change. There is continuity in the basic role of professors - to profess their subjects - and many of their duties would be recognised by their 19th century counterparts. But there is also change - in the increase in managerial responsibilities, in greater accountability and in the need to deal with the growing financial stringency.

But the greatest change has come in the nature of universities themselves. As early as 1973 Sir Charles Carter, the founding Vice-Chancellor of Lancaster University, was warning: "We have damaged the true cause of civilisation and culture by trying to convince people that universities are 'good business' and that education has a yield as good as that of a jam factory "[8] Lord Annan wrote in 1975: "The dons do not regard themselves as vocational teachers. They regard themselves as dedicated to the task of discovering new knowledge and redrawing the map of existing knowledge."[9] But they were already beginning to sound like voices from a previous age. The new egalitarian tone of society required a new rationale for universities and that was the idea of training people for specific jobs, precisely the utilitarian rationale that Newman had rejected.

---

[8] Higher Education 2 (1973) p 145.
[9] Stephens and Roderick eds, Universities for a Changing World, p 19

The change in the nature of universities and the role of academics within it was completed by the application to the system of the model of the free market - the Thatcherisation of the universities in the 1980s. This involved the transformation of the universities from communities of scholars into businesses, with the emphasis laid on vocational training, the inculcation of marketable skills, the reduction of state funding and the encouragement of private financing, and the importation of structures from America geared to facilitating customer choice. The wholesale upgrading of the polytechnics to university status signalled the direction of government higher education policy. The seal has been set on this transformation by the Dearing Report and the subsequent imposition upon students of tuition fees.

Robert Nisbet has suggested that the process of commercialisation began in America in the 1950s when universities which had previously shared the Newmanian ideal were overtaken by the higher capitalism, first in the natural sciences, then the social sciences and finally the humanities.[10] This led to the rise of 'the new men of power' - academic capitalists and professional entrepreneurs. So academics began to be appointed not for their abilities in teaching and research but for their money-raising and managerial capacities. Such figures often stood outside the traditional structures of the university, developing semi-autonomous fiefdoms, externally funded units that spearheaded the commodification of research. This has now begun to happen in Britain where, inconceivable a generation ago, it is possible to hear people referring to the university as 'the business' and students as 'the product'.

---

[10] Robert Nisbet, The Degradation of the Academic Dogma: the University in America 1945-70, London: Heinemann, 1971.

Some professors have embraced the new culture wholeheartedly and discovered hitherto unsuspected entrepreneurial skills. Others, of whom I am one, strenuously resist the imposition of the new philosophy. My own subject, history, teaches many useful skills: information gathering, problem solving, public presentation of arguments and assessments. But that should, in my view, be secondary to the broader objective of discovering how we were and how we got to where we are. It is not my purpose to turn out tunnel-visioned computer operators concerned only about where their next Porsche is coming from. I seek to awaken in my students an open-minded, broad-visioned humanity, informed by a love of learning, a love of ideas, a love of books, a love of argument and debate. An educated population is one of the glories of a civilised country and that should be the end and objective of university education.

However, the adoption of the commercial ethos means that what used to be a community of scholars, staff and students, engaged upon a common intellectual pursuit of intrinsic interest, value and coherence is in danger of being turned into a series of shambolic academic supermarkets in which student 'customers' load their trolleys haphazardly from pick 'n' mix shelves with cheap, nasty, flimsy modularised products lacking in intellectual fibre and spiritual nourishment. Recent structural changes in the nature of universities - modularisation, semesterisation, privatisation, commercialisation - are likely to mean the end of everything that has been distinctive about the British university system - classified degrees, small group teaching, the principle of intellectual maturation.

Perhaps the most pernicious development is the idea of the student as 'customer'. It is the antithesis of the previous system in which each teacher formed an individual pedagogical relationship with his/her students and each relationship was necessarily different and distinctive because of the different personalities, interests and intellectual goals of the people involved. The creation of the student 'customer' is already leading to a subtle shift in the relationship of professor and pupil. Whereas for generations, there has been an element of awe in the student attitude to the professor, that is in danger of being replaced by an element of fear in the attitude of professor to student. For under the new dispensation, the professor is required to sell himself and his course to the 'customer' and if he cannot recruit sufficient 'customers', there is a danger that he, his course, even his department may be for the chop.

Part of the process of commercialisation is the demystification of the professoriate. It is perfectly reasonable for 'customers' to ask and to be told - what does a professor do? For many, there will be two cultural images of the professor. One of them, hallowed by time, is that of the absent-minded professor, the 'prof' or 'boffin', a vague, unworldly, lovably dotty .figure, wrapped up in his work, dwelling in an ivory tower, quite likely to forget to turn up for lectures and given to asking students: "Was it you or your brother who was killed in the war?" It is the Alastair Sim/Margaret Rutherford image of the professor. The other, more recent image, is Malcolm Bradbury's Professor Howard Kirk, the ruthless smoothie, the cynical political operator, spending as much time bedding his students as teaching them. Both of these figures have been overtaken by events. The Alastair Sim/Margaret Rutherford professor has been forced into early retirement by academic restructuring and the change of priorities and the Howard Kirk professor is now seriously limited in his amorous activities by the strict codes of conduct laid down to govern relations between staff and students. So what does a professor in the 1990s do?

This collection of essays aims to give a snapshot of the life of the professor today, illustrating how professors are dealing with both the innovations and the continuities. Half of the contributors are from Lancaster University but the problems they address are universal and not specific to any one institution.

James Wright, Vice-Chancellor of Newcastle University, gives a wise and witty overview of the rise of the professoriate from the perspective of someone who has to deal with it on a day to day basis. Austin Woolrych recalls professorial life in the 1960s and before, an age now almost unimaginably remote. Many things have changed, both in society and in academia. But one thing which has not changed is the paucity of women in the professoriate - 8% at the last count. Johanna Laybourn-Parry explores this problem from the comparative perspective of Australia and Britain. Trevor Page reflects on the problems and predicaments facing the science professoriate. Three contributors address aspects of that administration which is now so prominent in the lives of professors. Ray Macdonald from a wealth of experience offers handy hints on how to survive as a head of department. Michael Newby gives an account of being a dean in a new university. John Clayton gives a Texan's view of that distinctive British activity - external examining - which consumes much professorial time and effort. But for all the general gloom about funding, administration and assessment, the true joy in academic life can still shine through, as it does in the essays by David Craig and Denis McCaldin on professing new subjects. As long as that joy remains both for those professing old subjects and those introducing new ones, the life of the professor will remain a fulfilling and rewarding one.

The Professoriate: Relentless Rise or Decline and Fall?

James Wright

Our language abounds with words which, like 'culture', have both a vague descriptive meaning and a rich emotive meaning. The descriptive meaning of them all is subject to constant redefinition. The words are prizes which each   man seeks to bestow on the qualities of his own choice.

C L STEVENSON: *Ethics and Language*

'Professor' is undoubtedly a word in this category, and so is constantly subject to what Stevenson calls 'persuasive definitions'.

I well remember a distinguished professor of theology (whose philosophical training should have taught him better) arguing passionately that every professor had a kind of divine right to be a member of the University Senate because they alone 'professed' their subject. With the intellectual insouciance which so often afflicts academics when they stray from their own subjects, he did not seem to be aware that by parity of reasoning he was depriving himself of the capacity to read or the need to lecture, these being activities presumably quintessentially reserved for Readers and Lecturers respectively.

That was over twenty years ago and the contemptuous Young Turk in me has been chastened by observing the move to the other end of the spectrum in the concept of what makes a professor. One now receives letters from competent middle-ranking people in a variety of walks of life, with whom one has been doing straightforward business for many years, but who have suddenly sprouted the word 'Professor' before or after their names - doubtless, one realises, on the strength of a few lectures or seminars they are giving on some vocational course in a university or college. The university has accorded the title 'Visiting Professor' as a gracious gesture (perhaps in lieu of more tangible reward), but hardly expected that it was permanently altering their public status.

For status is one of the most important things about being a professor. Despite the negative stereotypes - 'the mad professor', 'the absent-minded professor' - promoted by the philistinism of our popular culture, there has always been a general feeling that professors know a lot and deserve some respect for it. This is precisely the 'rich emotive meaning' which makes the title worth capturing for your own version of what being a professor is.

And 'knowing a lot' about some subject was once perhaps the main characterising feature of professors. It is only relatively recently that outstanding capacity in research has been widely seen as a necessary adjunct to the professor's knowledge of the subject. It is true that many professors did advance knowledge and did publish, and a total absence of publication might be regarded as unsatisfactory. But there was much more interest in the breadth and depth (by which I mean profundity rather than extreme specialisation) of their understanding of their field of study. The idea that you could be a professor of something like Early Nineteenth Century Moldavian Embroidery would have seemed absurd - the example is (so far as I know!) imaginary, but I could cite equally restricted cases from real life. You expected that professors would be able to discourse authoritatively on any aspect of their subject and would not dream of deploying the 'not my period' defence.

Deep knowledge of a subject is, however, no longer a sufficient condition for appointment as a professor - and, in some extreme cases, perhaps not even a necessary one. The expansion of individual universities and of the system and the recurring Research Assessment Exercises have changed everything. I can remember a colleague of the theologian's remarking that it was more pleasing to be granted a personal chair (then a great rarity) than an established one because she had not asked for it. Now, of course, established chairs are often filled by head-hunting people who would not dream of applying, and personal chairs are subject to personal application, often clamorous and sometimes with menaces.

The importance of being a professor, as opposed to some lower form of academic life, seems to have grown inversely to the general feelings of self-esteem in the academic profession and its perception of public recognition. When just to be a university teacher conferred some status in society - and a reasonably comfortable life style - and when professors were few in number, it was tolerable not to be one. This was notoriously so in Oxford and Cambridge, where academics of world class contentedly completed their careers as University Lecturers rather than become professors elsewhere. Even there it has now been found necessary to expand the number of Professorships (and Readerships) to satisfy the need for status. And, of course, the appetite feeds upon itself. The more professors there are the more unattractive it becomes not to have reached that level. But, inevitably, when it is not so distinctive to be a professor, the search for distinctions within the professoriate begins. Established professors are deemed to be more important than those who hold personal chairs. Among established professor there is now some interest in holding a 'named' chair, although we have not yet adopted the American fashion for 'Distinguished Professors' - what does that imply about the others?

I have indicated my suspicions about those who attempt to define what a professor is, but that is no bar to attempting a typology of modern professors and looking at some of their characteristics. There still is the most obvious class - people who are major authorities in their subject and who are capable in all sorts of ways, so that they are good teachers and managers as well. They look and act like the best kind of traditional professor. Happy is the Vice-Chancellor who is blessed with a good supply of this class - although also uneasy, because they are the most desirable targets in the transfer market. They carry with them not only the benefits of their own publications, but the capacity to lead and inspire others. The 'added value' that such people create is enormous.

Then there are those who are conspicuously successful in the current business of research - good at getting the grants in and the papers out. They may contribute only a limited amount in other fields and may, indeed, be rather selfish in their approach. They are the true beneficiaries of the RAE, particularly if they work in a highly competitive area and one in which the Funding Council unit of resource for research is high. You simply cannot afford to lose more than one or two of them, because the competition is to maintain or increase your share of a fixed pool of money. To lose someone is not only to reduce your own earning capacity but to increase someone else's. There has unquestionably been an increase in the numbers of people gaining chairs in these circumstances as opposed to Readerships or Senior Lectureships.

A third, and largely new, class consists of those who hold particular managerial office in Institutions of Higher Education - Deans, Pro Vice-Chancellors, Vice-Chancellors - and whose institutions believe they require to be dignified with the title of professor to do their job. This is a harmless affectation, but does create some degree of confusion in those who associate being a professor with a specifically academic activity grounded in a particular field of study. English usage tends to assume that if you are a professor you are a professor 'of' something, and it is not clear what these people are professors 'of'. It is not 'university management' (of which there doubtless are professors who make an academic study of it), any more than running a company makes someone a professor of management studies. A parallel group comprises the 'honorary' and 'visiting' categories to which I have already referred. If the title is seen as a courtesy one, no harm ensues. When it is assumed as a regular qualification it does no-one a service.

The multiplication of the number of professors and their types, combined with the growing complexity of universities as organisations, has created a crisis of identity for some professors. There was a time within living memory when to be a professor conferred not only status but power. You would probably also be head of department, either permanently or in rotation with one or two other similar barons - and I am referring to a period when the headship of a department was seen as a position worth having. No-one told you what to do and you told other people what to do and had considerable power over their lives and careers.

The democratisation of universities in the sixties weakened the professoriate from below. They had to pay attention to the views of junior colleagues or even students. They might find themselves outvoted or denied the headship of department. With many more professors in a department there was less likely to be an unquestioned leader, and, given the demands of modern administration for competence and attention to detail, the headship might fall upon someone who was not a professor.

In the eighties this nether millstone was joined by the new upper millstone of managerialism. You were expected to deliver what the head of department, the Dean, and the rest of the university hierarchy required. This has led to some of the bitterest feelings in the 'divine right' camp. One of my earliest tasks as a non-professorial member of the governing body of an ancient university in the seventies was to join a team examining the contract of every professor (and they varied widely) to see if we could actually compel them to do anything at all if they didn't want to. The issue of whether a head of department can require specific performance of a long-established professor (the contracts for recent appointments are different) is not a dead one.

So, while the economic power of some professors has been increased by the current climate of competition, others feel deprived of the significance to which they think their academic status entitles them. Hence the creation of professorial 'trade unions' to provide a distinctive voice in the debate on higher education. If they have something useful to say, we should all pay attention. It is hard, however, to see why in current circumstances they should be given a privileged hearing simply *because* they are professors. In this undeferential age it has to be what is said that counts, not who said it.

The history of the professoriate in the thirty-odd years that separate Robbins from Dearing might be seen, not surprisingly, as mirroring that of the institutions which they serve. They began the period few in number, in a position of some privilege, respected by society (although viewed as a little detached from that well-known fantasy of politicians and businessmen 'the real world'), and able to get on with their work, which they generally did very well, at their own pace. Now there are many more of them, and they are much more multifarious. They are less secure in their position within their own institution, and subject to more public criticism, although still relied on in a crisis - if you have a problem like BSE, you send for a professor. They work at a pace dictated by external pressures. As a class they have become more worldly, measuring success as much by air miles as ideas and relentlessly swapping business cards.

It is easy to caricature these changes, but just as there are now many more students, and of different kinds, enjoying the benefits of university education, and very enthusiastic about it, so the growth in the number and variety of professors has widened the scope and increased the excellence of the work that universities do. Professors may not be what they were, but that may not be a bad thing - even assuming that they ever were!

Happier Days

Austin Woolrych

What was it like, I am asked, to be a professor in the expansive sixties and seventies? There can be no one answer, because the job varied so much from university to university and from subject-area to subject-area. I write from my own experience as the first professor of history in the last of the six new English universities that were founded in the early 1960s under the impact of the Robbins Report. It was not a typical professorial career, but nor was the background from which I embarked on it.

By the time that Lancaster was appointing to chairs, Sussex, York, Warwick, East Anglia and Kent had taken their pick and there was a distinct sound of barrels being scraped. I was lucky to be short-listed, for my meagre list of publications would never have made me a candidate by today's standards. I had had to leave school early, without the equivalent of A-levels, and after four years in a dead-end job the state treated me to six and a half more of military service. But thanks to the war and a training scheme for its survivors, I went up to Oxford, and just three years after matriculating I was teaching history in Leeds University. By then I was over thirty, with a wife and two children, and I was registered for a BLitt; there could be no question of a doctorate, which would have required two further years' residence in Oxford. The research had to be done and the thesis written in the spare time left by a demanding teaching load before I could begin to write for publication; hence my slender CV when I applied to Lancaster.

The interview for the chair was held in a Bloomsbury hotel, and I did not think I performed well in it. When the taxi-driver who took me from it to a friend's house told me that President Kennedy had just been shot I took it as a bad omen. It came as no surprise, therefore, when the Vice-Chancellor telephoned me a week or two later to tell me that an internationally renowned historian (he named him, but I won't) was minded to come to Lancaster, and to wish me better luck next time. After another week or so, however, he rang again to say that the great man was 'making difficulties' (I never learned what they were), and that if I could drive over next day we could talk business. He took me out to one of the happiest lunches of my life, and so inaugurated the busiest and most rewarding part of it.

I had then no clear-cut model of a professor's role, for my fifteen years at Leeds had fallen in a transition period, and I had encountered a wide variety of specimens. Despots and dinosaurs were still around in academia, professors who ruled their departments by decree and had no truck with department meetings. They survived strongly in Wales and Scotland; Lucky Jim's boss had a real-life original who (I am informed) really did answer his office telephone with the words "History speaking". I myself, as external examiner, encountered another Welsh professor (English by birth) who used to hold a private meeting with his externals before the formal board of examiners and tell them what class of honours he thought each candidate should have, so as to obviate unseemly discussion. The only remotely comparable figures in the Faculty of Arts at Leeds were in the language and classics departments, though a neighbour of mine who had taught for many years in the medical school was compelled to couple his professor's name with his own as co-author of every article that he published, regardless of the said professor's actual input. In complete contrast my own first head of department, whom I remember with deep affection, was John Le Patourel, who took a personal interest in his staff's research projects, consulted them in regular meetings, encouraged their initiatives in devising new courses, and was on first-name terms with his most junior assistant lecturer - not a common practice among professors fifty years ago. He greatly extended the teaching of undergraduates in small groups, so that no lecture course was without its tutorial back-up, and he took a full share of the teaching load himself. I later realised how fortunate I had been when A J P Taylor talked to me (uncomplainingly) of the slave-driving to which he had been subjected when he first taught at Manchester, only twenty years or so before I began at Leeds. From his very first year he had to prepare and deliver a staggering weekly stint of lectures, covering centuries and continents, and he felt that he had to make them good because they were the only teaching that his students would get.

What made taking up a chair in a new university so different from succeeding to one in a well established department was that all kinds of basic things had to be decided at great speed, without the consultation with colleagues that one would have ideally wished. There was no leisurely period of planning for Lancaster's founding fathers; I finished my last course at Leeds in May 1964 and began my first one in Lancaster in October. One of the first things to be done was to devise a syllabus, because much as I should have liked to discuss it with my departmental staff a prospectus had to go to press before any of them were appointed. An Academic Planning Board consisting of senior academics from other universities had laid down the basic structure of Lancaster's degrees, and a 'Shadow Senate' met several times from January 1964 onward to take urgent practical decisions of policy, but what was to be taught in particular subjects lay very much with the original professor to determine.

Giving a first shape to the syllabus was one of the great challenges and privileges of starting up a new department; another, still greater, was selecting its staff. It expanded at a greater rate than I or anyone else had envisaged, thanks to Lancaster's practice of requiring first-year students to take three subjects of equal weight and permitting them to major in any of these in which they perform well enough, regardless of which they originally applied for. Since the first-year history courses were unconventional and stimulating, we regularly recruited more students for Part II than we had admitted to Part I. The university always allocated additional staff where there was a demonstrable teaching need, and the growth was phenomenal, from a strength of four in 1964/5 to 29 ten years later. In one year alone we made six new appointments, simply to meet the demands of teaching. This was immensely exciting, but it involved a lot of work, including writing to well over 100 referees before making our short lists, and then interviewing 20-odd candidates. The fields seemed to get better from year to year, apart from a paucity of good women candidates, for in those happy days graduates with good degrees and a taste for academic life could embark on doctorates in the confidence of DES support and in good hope of a university post at the end of the line. In sad contrast, for four years running in the mid-nineties more than half the holders of first class honours who have applied for grants to support them through further degrees in the humanities and social sciences have been turned down for lack of funds.

The encouragement to innovate, the freedom to expand into new areas of study and the confidence that resources would be found to support worthy initiatives were among the things that made a professor's life so rewarding thirty years ago. I found a special stimulus in Lancaster's early years in the youth and enthusiasm of my departmental colleagues, for by the time we appointed them most of the experienced teachers in older universities who wanted a change had found a niche in one of the other new places. Only one in nine of those who joined us in the first ten years were scholars in mid-career, though the help that I received from these relative veterans (the oldest was 41 on appointment) was of great value. The majority were in their first post, and the rest had at most two or three years' experience elsewhere. So although my ideal was a democratic department, whose head's main job would be to articulate its collective will, a degree of tactful leadership was called for in the early years - at least I hope it was tactful. Whatever my colleagues thought of it, and various in temperament though they were, they shared a gift for laughter and a determination to make their department one of the best in the country.

Teaching and other departmental duties were of course only part of a professor's workload, especially in a new university. So much that runs in grooves in older places had to be worked out as we went along, and the process took years. Senate meetings were long, committees numerous and time-consuming, and though representatives from every level of the university community were brought into the decision-making process, the brunt fell on the founding professors. Much of this work was absorbing, for instance meeting our architects regularly in the buildings committee when our first permanent buildings were still going up, defining the relationship between colleges and departments, and arguing the pros and cons of continuous assessment. It was stimulating to be the first chairman of the equivalent of a faculty board, and I never grudged the Saturday mornings I gave to chairing the library committee through two three-year stints. I never thought to see the day when financial stringency would force the library to suspend the purchase of books.

The great difficulty was to find time enough for all these activities while carrying out one's teaching and keeping up one's research. The problem became acute during the wave of student unrest that in Lancaster reached its peak in 1970-2. The movement was a national, indeed an international one, stemming as it did from spectacular demonstrations in Paris in 1968. Its organisers found fertile ground in the new universities, and Lancaster, with its high proportion of resident students and its somewhat inward-looking community, sited three miles outside a smallish town, was very vulnerable. It survived a much publicised row in 1968 about the proposed non-segregation of the sexes in one of its colleges without serious disruption, but in 1970 it was hit by the growingly familiar tactics of sit-ins, demonstrations, boycotts of classes in some departments, and occasional violent interruptions of meetings of the Senate and Council. The issues were seldom specific to Lancaster except in one case when a member of staff was nearly dismissed; the first occupation of the Senate Room was occasioned by events at the LSE, the next wave by the alleged misuse of student records at Warwick, and the last of the series by Bloody Sunday in Londonderry. In the worst episodes the whole administration block and the computer room were occupied by demonstrators, seriously disrupting the running of the university for weeks at a time. (In one important respect things are better now than then, for students in general are more responsible and more committed to serious study, even though financial constraints subject them to greater poverty and compel the university to offer them less. All credit to them.) In 1971 I was elected Pro-Vice-Chancellor, one of three, and since I had special responsibility for student and college affairs I was right in the firing line. The many emergency meetings and constant negotiations took a heavy toll in time and stress, and at my colleagues' own suggestion I reduced my teaching load during my four years of office.

At the same time I remarked how well my department was running while I was too preoccupied to fuss over it, and after presiding over it for ten years I followed the example of several other departments and put the headship into rotation. I confess that I was still enjoying the role, for it was so much pleasanter then than now. Everyone felt secure in his or her job and optimistic about the future. We had enough staff to teach in the way we felt right, and we were not distracted in it by over-busy investigation. As head, I was not overburdened with paperwork or financial administration, and I always had sufficient clerical assistance. I was not required to measure my colleagues' research output in coffeespoons for some external scoresheet; I found that a commitment to research was better maintained by the healthy rivalry among bright young scholars and by the example and interest of their more senior colleagues. Those whose productivity caused slight concern could be numbered on the fingers of one hand of an accident-prone sawmill worker, and they were exceptionally effective teachers. There was room for them too.

My second ten years at Lancaster were scarcely less rewarding than my first, and they were certainly more relaxed. Nevertheless, I count myself as lucky in the time of my retirement as in that of my appointment. By 1983 the tide of expansion was on the ebb, financial stringency was beginning to bite, and people doing a good job and still enjoying it were coming under pressure to retire early. Personally I had nothing to grumble about, I took my pay-off at 65 instead of 67, but continued to teach what I enjoyed teaching for two more years. Nor am I lamenting any general decline in the status or function of professors. There was never a justification for assuming that scholars and scientists who had distinguished themselves in research would necessarily be skilled administrators or gifted in drawing the best out of a team of colleagues. It was never a good idea to vest permanent and unlimited authority over a department in one person, nor was it healthy that a university's academic governing body should consist simply of its senior executive officers and its professoriate. Professors, I believe, should always be prepared to carry positions of responsibility at departmental, faculty or university level, but should not be entitled to them *ex officio*. There are currently seven professors in my old department, and if I were still in post I would be happy with any of them as head, but the present excellent head is not a professor. She therefore represents it on the Senate, on which professors sit only if they have positive functions as heads of departments, deans, principals of colleges or (possibly) elected representatives of specific constituencies. All this strikes me as right and proper, not only in the interests of democracy but because professors should be encouraged to devote most of their time to their essential roles, which I take to be advancing the frontiers of knowledge in their subject, representing its interests in the wider world of learning, and passing on their skills to the next generation of scholars and scientists. As for the gardening professors whom Bruce Truscot memorably pilloried in Redbrick University, and who, once promoted, cultivated their rhododendrons while resting on their laurels, they were a species whose extinction will not be mourned.

It seems fair to say that what has been done over the past fifty years to reform the functions of professors has been effected by the universities themselves, whereas most of the things that have made academic life less attractive in the last twenty-odd have been forced on them from outside. It is the whole profession that has suffered, and if professors have felt it more than most it is because most of them are old enough to have seen better times; financially they have been better able to bear the erosion of salaries. Nearly thirteen years have passed since I taught my last seminar, so I know of the deteriorating conditions of service mainly at second-hand. But they do arise mainly through government's determination to squeeze a little more out of the universities each year, in return for a little less funding in real terms. It is sad that a worsening of the staff-student ratio has forced a steady increase in the size of tutorial groups; sadder still that subjects like classics and philosophy and the study of languages and literatures other than our own are going to the wall, while resources are channelled into vocational skills of immediate commercial application. I have nothing against business schools, but the balance does seem to have gone awry. And I am disturbed by the constant checks on performance which rob my old colleagues of time that they would rather devote to their essential professional functions, in order presumably to satisfy far-off efficiency experts whose criteria may yield dividends in the commercial world but are less apposite to a community of scholars. But what depresses me most of all when I talk to former colleagues, in my own subject and in others, is the general fall in their morale and their despondency about the future of universities.

The bright spot in this rather dark picture is that there is little that cannot quickly be remedied by a restoration of adequate funding, but in the current climate there are not enough votes in higher education to make this a likely prospect. Is it starry-eyed to hope that our politicians may come to care more for the nurseries of science and the training-grounds of the nation's future teachers and administrators? For professors, the essential concern should be that nothing divides them from the rest of the academic community in the struggle that lies ahead.

No Peace

David Craig

As it happens, a few days before I sat down to write this piece I had come back to my old room at Lancaster to take three workshops with undergraduates and postgraduates in Creative Writing. This had been my work for twelve years until semi-retirement in 1994, and for eighteen years before that if you change 'workshops' to 'seminars' and 'Creative Writing' to 'English Literature'. For six hours this year, then, I was reminded of the absorbing interest, the verbal richness, and the sheer pleasure of such work.

An American student with a Japanese name 'defended' his long and subtle story with the resource of an experienced intellectual and also with a charming amusedness as he relished over again his trio of crazy characters on their spaced-out trip through the Middle West. Another American explained that her poem 'Wake', a vivid lament for what drugs do to the brain, took its title from the Californian phrase 'wake and bake' - to wake up and smoke some pot. This sparked off a lively conversation about the flow of idioms to and fro across the Atlantic. ('Sorted' is not yet understood over there and a Portuguese student reminded us that *Trainspotting* needed sub-titles when it was screened, with great success, in the US.)

A woman who came, I think, from Merseyside, wearing a small gold stud in her nose, explained that her close-packed monologue about a girl 'off the estate', who comes up against every kind of squalid privation and class-prejudice in her young life, was one of twelve meant for radio. A youngish poet, a Lancaster graduate who I knew to have been writing to near-Faber standard for at least two years, explained how he wanted to improve his already amazing poem about a visionary house of ice which starts to thaw and dislimn.

None of the work I saw, from twenty students, was dull. Some of it was clumsy and faulty. All of it was intensely stimulating in the originality with which it had been imagined. We were discussing it in order to evaluate its quality - to find out how, and how well, it worked; to suggest sharpenings, deepenings, and eliminations in the texts; to see how far they had realised the potential of their writers' ideas; to come up with suggestions on how the work might be developed. We followed up affinities with other writers. All this struck me once again as educative in the most fruitful and the least routine-bound sense. Chekhov was invoked, as the European pioneer of the 'unfinished' ending; Brecht, as a master exponent and theorist of the poetic line, whether run-on or end-stopped; Peter Fonda's film *Easy Rider*, as a classic of the road movie, the story of a trip in both main current senses. I do believe that our conversations were both academic, in that they drew on and added to literary knowledge, and artistic, in that they helped bring into being and improve new poetry and fiction.

By now you must be thinking that either I have a swelled head or else I am dangerously euphoric; also, that there must be a catch, and it is high time I introduced it. Well yes, there is. This subject, Creative Writing, now has ninety students at Lancaster, from Part I to PhD, and at least twelve sister departments exist in the higher education sector. We have a long record of thrifty management and academic success: twenty-eight years' experience at Lancaster; a 4 in the ratings; and numerous publications under the best auspices by staff and students. The subject still lacks the status of department. It had no titular head with a permanent full-time post until last year. It has had to struggle for some years now to find a home:

first, nowhere; then with Theatre Studies in the School of Creative Arts; then nowhere again when that School folded after some years of fitful half-life; then Independent Studies - and that too will turn into nowhere if some of the latest threats of 'restructuring', ie closing-down, are carried out.

"There is no peace and rest in the development of material interests," says Dr Monygham in the final section of Conrad's Nostromo. There is no peace and no rest in academe these days, because we are being forced incessantly to appraise, assess, validate, monitor, measure, report - in a word, to manage. Our very old national culture, with its 300-year-old central bank and stock exchange and its 330-year-old civil service, has now added to its stupefyingly elaborate system of paper-mongering a new, Thatcherised accountability which is scarcely bearable. And it will always be there now, because the only way to reform it would be - to ask the consultants and officials to appraise, monitor and measure still more, in order to tweak and tune the system in a thousand tortuous ways. They set the agenda, from Whitehall downwards, and they will never strip down their system and remake it on humane and bearable lines because that would shrink their own roles and very likely put paid to their own jobs.

I could not bear - even if I could wave a time-wand and run history backwards - to remove the Emeritus from my present title and become a fully active professor and departmental leader again, because it would force me to spend perhaps one-third of my time and more than half my mental capacity drawing up plans and 'mission statements'; budgeting; delivering 'narratives' of my department's work and the wonderful achievements of its staff; and gearing up for and undergoing assessments and appraisals. For this is now the age when an experienced and productive scholar in a modern languages department must *do no research for an entire term* so that she can be free to organise and write her department's submission for the Research Assessment Exercise. Which is itself a mockery because staff members can score points by entering books written before they joined the university, so people with lots of publications to their name are headhunted for the points they will score for their new work-place! This is the age when a member of the administration can do nothing for months on end but coach staff on how to shine at the said Exercise.[11] In spite of all this self-criticism the true value and ethos of education still eludes our monitors. When Creative Writing was about to undergo Academic Appraisal, we were at first not asked to demonstrate teaching ability and the assessors only sat in on live workshops at our request. Can it be that the new power-players have no respect for teaching? When Creative Writing at another institution, down south, was inspected by the Higher Education Funding Council assessors, the lecturers (who are excellent poets and novelists) found that they were being judged by a panel who did not practise creative writing themselves, had never taught it, and have never been taught it. (They recommended - more theory, more mission statements, and fewer workshops.) Can it be that the power-players have no respect for original uses of language and how these may be nurtured in apprentice writers by good teachers?

What makes me gnash and squirm all the more is that this rack on which we are all being strained to pieces is not just academic, it is nation-wide, civilisation-wide. Examples spring to hand from every walk of life. Two from The Guardian for February 8: Scotland's only female penal facility, Cornton Vale Prison near Stirling, has seen six suicides and seven serious attempts in two years, after many years with no such

---

[11] A military term, like 'task force', 'flagship', and other items of Eighties and Nineties academic slang.

trouble. One of the chief causes mentioned by those running Cornton is "too much paperwork flying around for the system to work properly." The BBC's most distinguished producer, Kenith Trodd, has just been sacked after saying in a lecture to the National Film Theatre that "writers were no longer free to do their own thing"; decisions were being taken by "uncreative people whose talent is keeping a shaky grip on stationery supplies." The police say they can't spend enough time on the streets because they have to write so many reports. My eldest son, a Senior Research Officer at the DSS, told me some years ago that the new system of contracting-out the fact-finding jobs to do with benefit payments had led in one case to 139 tenders being received from private agencies for a single job. So 138 of them were so much wasted time and paper!

Our civilisation is strangling itself with financial-managerial systems. Some years ago I read that quantities of the most expensive weapons in America remain in their crates on the bases because they are so complicated that only their inventors understand them and the operating manuals are impossibly complicated. Ordinary fitters haven't a chance. No doubt the weapons were commissioned by a quango loaded with retired generals and admirals, with a budget supervised by accountants. It's no better on the campus. Three years ago, as I recall, the secretaries in our Humanities faculty (all of them, in my experience, devoted and intelligent) sent round a heartfelt letter about the new and very expensive Prophesy accounting system which Lancaster had just bought: they would dearly like to make it work, only they hadn't been given any instruction in it, or preparation for its arrival, so now they were expected to couch their departmental budgets in a code for which none of them had been trained. Why had nobody thought of that? Because the all-powerful accountants and consultants no longer have any conception of what goes on in normal offices and teaching-rooms.

The secretaries would love to run their departments efficiently. We teachers would like to give our whole minds to teaching and research (which in Creative Writing means mainly writing poems, stories, novels and scripts). Our real work is (1) to converse interestingly and intelligently in the workshops about the students' latest draft poems and fictions, in a manner adjusted sensitively to the thirty or forty very different people to pass weekly through each of our rooms; and (2) to keep space in our heads in which our own visions and memories will remain available for the next time when we have two or three days free to compose them into our own poems and fictions, scripts and essays. Now, on top of those, the system demands that we constantly redefine, justify, and reorganise our educational practice in financial and numerical terms that will satisfy a regiment of power-players driven by two motive-forces - 'value for money' and the continuance of their own jobs.

It is all a horrible shame. When I took over the teaching of Creative Writing at Lancaster (building on what I had set up with Anne Cluysenaar and Frank Goodridge in the English Department in 1969), I tried to keep it limber, practical, true to the art itself. No lectures; no exams or tests; no set assignments; no bibliographies; no limit on the amount written (and no minimum either: only a couple of students over the decades have written too little). Most writers are well read; they are not usually systematic scholars. Most writers work to commission; their work is in the first place their own conception, *then* it is made the subject of a contract which stipulates wordage, form, and theme. The publisher who gave me my real launch into national publication, David Godwin at Secker (who finally left publishing in despair at the crass, money-driven policies of his bosses at Random House), said to me at one of our first meetings, "I don't believe in getting the marketing people to come up with an idea, then finding an author to carry it out. Good books come from the writer." This has been the principle behind the extremely open or permissive curriculum of our subject at Lancaster, and I do believe it worked. It still does - inside the teaching rooms; but erosion has set in. How can one person (my successor) be a writer *and* a teacher *and* a manager? Why must we splinter our powers and our concentration in the effort to maintain the integrity of the unit in the teeth of these tendencies to administer it out of existence because it's too small, or can't be fitted into the Finance Office's computer programmes, or because bosses with little or no feeling for teaching and writing want to lump us together with some incongruous subject instead of letting us do our own thing?

The living arts - film-making, musical composition, sculpture, writing stories, or whatever - have not been present in academe for very long and I have done my best to help them make themselves at home there. Most recently, when the School of Creative Arts was still alive, I was madly optimistic enough to believe that living arts were coming into their own at Lancaster on the strength partly of the staff seminars which we were running. Twice a term teachers of music, art, theatre, and creative writing met to hear one of us talk about and demonstrate our current research projects. The conversations, the spirit of the exchanges, the intensity of the intellectual and aesthetic interest remain among my happiest and most inspiring memories since I began working here in June 1964, whether the topic was the *zeitgeist* audible in a Mahler symphony, or non-figurative sculpture, or photographs made in homage to Victorian botanical prints, or the role of accident in verbal and visual art, or the fieldwork carried out in a world-wide exploration of great rocks. After several years of delicious co-operation, the programme lapsed, explicitly because colleagues no longer felt free or able to add this 'extra' to their crushing burden of new managerial tasks.

It was not an extra. It was how a university should work. It was bound to be stifled and killed off by the managerial-Thatcherite ethos with its systems, its paperwork, its incessant restructuring, and the whole Chinese torture known as Death by a Thousand Cuts.

How to survive as Head of Department

Ray Macdonald

First experiences

It was my second or third day as Head of Department (HoD). The paper work quota for the day was finished. Time to put the feet up onto the desk and do some visionary thinking about where the subject was going and how we intended to stay at the forefront. The office door imploded and in stormed a cleaning lady, formidable beyond her early twenties. "What are you going to do about the toilet roll holders in the men's toilets?" She saw the lack of an immediate response as a sign of weakness and proceeded to give me a fifteen minute harangue on the iniquities of life on the cleaning staff.

That was my first experience of one of the more important roles of the HoD - to be a listening ear whilst a staff member vents his or her anger or frustration. Commonly no interjection is required, just patience until the injustices are righted in the speaker's mind. He or she departs in a more relaxed mood and a potential glitch in the smooth running of the department has been avoided. Being the recipient of other people's unhappiness is, however, wearing and accumulative, and I found myself increasingly unable to deal sympathetically with what were usually minor problems.

Whatever the pressures, I did not break my prime rule - never lose your temper. When I have seen it happen to senior colleagues, I have invariably felt that it demeaned them. Other HoDs feel differently, one colleague told me that she used loss of temper, very rarely, as a shock tactic. She claimed spectacular results as grown men were rendered speechless.

Where does it all begin?

Most universities will have a formal description of how HoDs are chosen, for example, by departmental vote, by dictate of the Faculty Dean or even of the Vice-Chancellor (in exceptional control-freak cases). It is difficult to get at the truth - nobody would ever admit to wanting to be HoD, even though he or she has spent months priming the Dean about a willingness to sacrifice self for the common good. I suspect that there are three main methods for choosing HoDs:

The good soldier This is the acceptance that it is a moral obligation of the professoriate to be HoD at some stage and "Regrettably, I am currently Buggins". Skilful Deans will easily spot candidates with this in-built weakness.

Entrapment If Buggins refuses to do his or her turn, Buggins or some other candidate may be offered inducements, such as the continued employment of a post-doc or teaching assistant, or the promise of a full year's sabbatical at the end of the Headship period. Few universities seem to employ the obvious, but presumably *de trop*, method of making the HoD allowance even moderately attractive.

Wishful thinking Some professors may see the Headship as a step towards greater administrative things, such as the Deanship or even *(sotto voce)* a Pro Vice-Chancellorship. This is a high risk route, since there is little evidence that VCs consider being HoD as a useful training for anything much.

What do you have to do?

The recent expansion of the UK university system, without commensurate increase in funding, plus the seemingly endless round of research and teaching assessments, are necessitating significant changes in our working methods. All institutions are struggling to cope with these changes. Long-term planning, at all levels from the VC's office to the departmental, is increasingly difficult as we respond to external and internal demands for mission statements, student statistics or whatever, at, commonly, a few days or weeks notice. Last year, as we followed a major internal audit by preparations for the HEFCE Teaching Quality Assessment, a colleague in Biological Sciences remarked to me that it you pull a plant up often enough to look at its roots, it will die. I confessed to feeling distinctly dehydrated around the radicles.

Against this background of continuing change, the role of HoD has become increasingly confused. Some universities, including my own, have established committees to try to define the requirements of the post. Almost all recommendations involve increased resources which are not available in financially stringent times.

Part of the problem in producing a generalised description is that the job is highly variable. Take, for example, the Heads of a Humanities and a Science department. They will require many skills in common - the ability to manage and encourage staff, the wisdom of Solomon in allocating teaching and administrative duties, the strength of character to represent the department at Faculty and higher levels, the patience to communicate with central administration, a clear vision of the shape, development and research profile of their department, and the energy to cope with the endless audits.

There are, though, many differences. The Humanities Head will not normally have to manage a (possibly large) technical staff, a large resident population of research staff and students and a complex and expensive suite of laboratories. The scale of the job is different; the Head of a modestly sized science department can easily have responsibility on a day-by-day basis for 150 people.

A major area of responsibility for the science head is safety. New legislation is placing increasing burdens on the universities and these are, necessarily, passed down to HoD level. I have personal experience of being told, in most forcible terms, by an officer of the Health and Safety Executive that I could be in danger of litigation if certain improvements to our safety procedures were not carried out promptly. And this, I may say, in a department which took safety issues extremely seriously.

Finally, there is normally a major difference in the financial budgets. During several years of my Headship, our annual turnover exceeded £2.5 million, of which about half was external income. There were hundreds, perhaps thousands (I didn't dare check), of individual transactions, ranging from a box of test tubes to spectrometers worth over £100k. Many institutions have attempted some form of financial devolution, whereby departments take responsibility for the sound management of their budgets. Whilst this affords a measure of flexibility and freedom in budgeting, it may also be a nightmare for someone who is not trained in financial management.

I looked forward rather eagerly to one HoD duty - attending Senate. At last a chance to find out how the university really works and perhaps to contribute in some small way. I sat beside a colleague with whom I had played cricket for the staff team some years previously. "Rule number one, laddie. Always take some work to do at Senate; some letters to write, a book to review. Best place I know for a bit of peace and quiet." Cynical, but regrettably true. Our Senate is simply too large to be truly effective. It reflects a major conundrum for universities; where is the balance between democratic representation and effective action? How flat can your administrative structure be when external pressures are most easily responses to by a pyramidal governance?

What makes a good HoD?

There is no template of a successful HoD. It is a complex function of personality and ambition. Some HoDs adopt the managerial approach, delegating every duty that can possibly be delegated but maintaining the role of ultimate arbiter. Others, in need perhaps of the moral high ground, get involved in every aspect of departmental business. Some drop all teaching, others carry heavy teaching loads. Some forego personal research, others take the opportunity to pursue it more vigorously. Ultimately, the most important criterion of the success of a HoD is, "Is the departmental prospectus in research and teaching being delivered?"

I think, though, that all good HoDs understand the need for constant communication with their staff. I found that if people were privy to how decisions were made and were allowed to comment on the process, they were usually willing to accept the decisions, no matter how unpalatable. It is also important that HoDs get their facts right, well in advance of meetings, whether at the individual or staff meeting level. It is, I suppose, a matter of simple trust.

It also helps to be a little street-wise, in the sense of understanding what motivates individuals and how they present themselves. I soon learned that when Dr X slid into my office, full of bonhomie and consideration for my welfare, he wanted money for something. Professor Y's jovial acquiescence to almost anything you put to him was followed by an almost total failure to do any task that he found uninteresting. To be able to predict someone's reaction to a given situation gives you the opportunity to be forearmed.

What do you do with 'difficult' academic staff?

This is one of the most contentious issues which a new HoD will have to face. There is a consensus that every department has some staff members who are unco-operative, who do not pull their weight, or who do not share in the current vision of the department's future. There is no consensus as to what constitutes the evidence for this view. The main culprit is the vagueness of the academic contract, which implicitly acknowledges that research creativity cannot be predicated on a 9 to 5 basis and that *excellence* in teaching cannot be imparted.

If the HoD decides, therefore, to question formally the performance of a particular member of staff, he or she will be faced with a major stumbling block - where is the written statement of what, in detail, is expected or required? Confrontation on this basis is usually pointless. I preferred to try to get the best out of the staff involved, arguing that it is better to get 50% effort rather than virtually none from someone who is totally disenchanted. Future HoDs will have the advantage of more tightly written contracts for staff as universities address the problem of quantifiable performance indicators. They will still, however, have to acknowledge the fact that academic creativity cannot be manufactured and that every staff member will produce at different rates and in different styles.

Perks of the job?

Are there, indeed, any perks of the job? Of course there are:

- Being associated with the department's achieving a high research rating or an excellent in teaching
- The pleasure of a colleague for whom you have successfully negotiated a promotion
- The sense of repaying the system which has given you a job which, despite increasing problems, never fails to stimulate by giving you enormous scope for following teaching and research lines which are innovative and rewarding.

For me, one of the most enjoyable aspects of the job was in strengthening my interest in undergraduate teaching. It may have been partly age-related; my daughters were both at university and I thus had considerable empathy for the students. It was also a response to their enthusiasm, their camaraderie and their trust that you were delivering to them a course of which they could be proud. I would be less than strictly honest if I did not admit that spending an afternoon in a teaching laboratory was also a sweet way of getting away from the desk and the admin chores.

One of the more taxing experiences of being Head was in having to deal with visiting students from northern European universities. They seemed to have a greater ability to see through what is termed in modern youth parlance, I believe, as bullshit, and were very efficient at seeing any gap between what was promised for a course and what was actually being delivered. One German student, in particular, was able to make me feel distinctly uncomfortable as I attempted to explain why Dr X's coursework still had not been marked and returned to them, or why students could not have access to the building after 6.00 pm.

Handy hint for Heads

I would say that the main aim of the HoD should be to create and maintain for your colleagues a working environment which is stimulating, progressive, exciting, flexible, personally rewarding and *good-humoured*. I particularly stress the last point; get the atmosphere right and the department will look after itself.

Being a Dean

Michael Newby

Being a Dean in a new university is not like being a Dean in an old one. You aren't, for instance, voted in by colleagues for a three-year stint, afterwards to fall back with relief into the library to resume your research. It's a full-time, permanent management post, usually 'third-tier', senior to everyone except the Vice-Chancellors and their Deputies. Deans run Faculties. They may also carry cross-institutional responsibilities: mine are to be a member of the University's Executive (Vice-Chancellor and Deputies, Deans and Divisional Heads) and to chair its Teaching and Learning Policy Committee.

Most of our professors are researchers whose work justifies the label which proclaims that they profess their discipline at its highest level. Many Deans also carry the title 'Professor' and some may do so by virtue of their research. Others, myself included, carry it more as an honorific, the post I applied for not having been advertised as a research post. The justification, I suppose, is that anyone who achieves what it takes to become a Dean is, by definition, 'distinguished' enough to warrant the title. I like the versatility of the 'new' universities in their preparedness to admit other people as professors than only those who are eminent researchers. However, I fear that, as the differences between 'new' and 'old' begin to blur, research is becoming the only criterion which really seems to count. Though our professors mix the various ingredients of distinction (teaching, management, track-record, etc) in different measures, most overwhelm the other flavours with the piquancy of their research.

What's more, though some may pull it off, I don't believe it's possible for many of us to be both Deans and significant researchers at the same time. The work-load is heavy; though moving through seasonal changes, it is unremitting; and its nature means that one must be prepared for constant interruptions, unexpected deadlines, sudden crises. I long ago learned that the occasional 'empty' day in the diary was the most dangerously deceptive of all, for it is invariably the one in which such crises occur. Were I to spend, say, half my time pensive and curious in the Library, my Faculty would cease to function. (At least I hope it would.)

The day-job, then, is running the Faculty. Some numbers here may be helpful, to get a sense of the scale of the thing. My faculty (Arts & Education) operates on two of the University's four campuses, together with two city-centre annexes, ten miles apart from each other and sixty miles from head office. We teach some 2,500 full-time undergraduates in three modular degree programmes, together with about a hundred students on our PGCE. At postgraduate, post-experience level, we have close to 1,300 students on modular part-time routes which can lead to Masters. We have approaching 50 MPhil/PhD students. We have distant oversight of about another thousand students working at diploma or undergraduate level on franchised programmes in other institutions. A hundred or so students a year study with us from countries abroad. We employ about 120 academic staff, together with part-time staff (everyone from visiting professors to life-models) counted not as separate genetic entities but as 'part time hours', so I don't know how many there are. We have around 35 administrative staff and 25 technicians. It is a large undertaking costing many millions a year, money for which I am responsible (and ultimately sackable if I get it wrong).

I run the Faculty with a senior team consisting of four Heads of School (who also take whole-Faculty responsibilities), and Heads of Research and Faculty Administration. I also bring three members of the non-promoted lecturing staff on to the Faculty Executive on a two- or three-year rotation in order to ensure that there's a 'grass-roots' influence in our decision-making. All the academic decisions are taken in committees and boards with elected representatives working alongside the *ex-officio* members (those who have to be there by virtue of their position within the Faculty).

That's the width: what of the quality? One way to describe what I actually do is to say that I *preside over* (the verb is probably not a perfect expression of reality) the process of recruitment, induction, teaching, assessment and graduation of all our students; over the appointment, appraisal, development and sometimes promotion of all our staff; over the management and distribution of all our money and our other resources; and over the allocation and safety management of all our teaching space (though I don't carry responsibility for the estates themselves, nor for their upkeep and maintenance, nor for the central services - like Library, catering, residence, etc - which attend the functions of each Faculty). I preside over the formulation, management and outcome of our research; over the curriculum; over the syllabuses; over the way we organise ourselves into groupings of various kinds to do various jobs; over the quality assurance processes; over our relationships with the rest of the University, and with the other educational agencies with which we work. I preside over the many rhetorics and arguments, disagreements and alliances which make up a large and complex sub-organisation within the University. I am supposed to offer the words which will best express to others our many purposes, and in this sense I preside over the Faculty's 'philosophy'. I preside over its people, inasmuch as a great deal of my time is spent in knowing about and trying to assist staff. I preside over its morale.

'Preside over' because, of course, I don't do all these things myself, but I have to ensure that someone else does, and must also be satisfied that they do them well. In fact, I try to encourage other people to do as many of them as possible. But Deans here are supposed to be in charge of all this, and if things go wrong then ultimately it's they who must accept responsibility.

Deans also initiate. I'm never quite convinced that one of the laws of clever management is to make people think it was their idea all along (though sometimes that works well, and often is also happens to be true). If Deans never had any ideas of their own, I suspect people would quickly wonder what they drew their salaries for. But having ideas is only the start of the process: it's much harder to get people to support them, and then move them into a realised, practical reality. Time can sometimes be important here: when my faculty was first formed (as the result, four years ago, of two faculties merging) I spent the first three months consulting widely among its members on how we should organise ourselves, deciding upon a School structure. One of the Schools (consisting of a wide range of disparate subjects) was difficult to name, and eventually I chose *Humanities & Cultural interpretation.* "After all," said one member of staff, "interpreting the culture is what we all do, isn't it?" I always hoped that the 'cultural interpretation' idea would move further than just to exist as the second half of a title, at the time believing that the processes of interpreting our own and other cultures was complex, compelling, difficult and worthy of study. Four years on, groups of people in that School, working with others in the Faculty, are beginning to plan a new degree pathway, probably to be called *Cultural Interpretation & Practice.* This

- if it comes off - is a good example of initiating unobtrusively - and patiently.

Deans also react. Having teacher education as a significant part of my Faculty means that we react on a twice-weekly basis, these days, to the latest consultation document from the Teacher Training Agency or OFSTED. We often ask why we bother, for the good it does, but like the party you don't want to go to, but feel you have to be seen at, so with these documents: we feel we should respond for fear that, one day, their worst excesses may come to haunt us if we don't. Certainly, teacher education is currently the most embattled part of higher education, as government quangos do their best to suffocate it with perverse bureaucracy. Our response strategy reminds me of those gardeners working at the turn of the century on the Great Estate who ensured that their asparagus beds were *perfectly* aligned, at an angle of *exactly* 45°, as a way of showing their contempt for the man for whom they worked and the aristocratic system he represented. Find the fault in *that*, you bastards, but don't think it makes the slightest difference to the taste of the asparagus!

Higher education is a process, marked along the way by a series of products. Deans profess to understand how this process works, and how they can coerce it to the benefit of those they manage and represent. The products are what testify to their ability, or otherwise, to influence the process. There are a great many products: numbers of students recruited successfully to target; quality of their degree outcomes; amount of money earned from sources other than the funding council (research grants, QR money, etc); staff who gain promotion, within or outside the institution; PhD completions; good examiners' reports ... these are regulars. Also countable are the absence of things: a low complaints count from people in the neighbourhood about students' street behaviour is one; from those within the Faculty about anything at all another; low drop-out rates a third. We live in a world where worth is counted in measures like these, and Deans are held responsible.

Yet the real values are more definable in terms of the processes over which Deans preside. Do people feel they have somewhere to go with good ideas? Is morale high or low? Are our academic freedoms defended when attacked? Are our standards high? What do visitors to the Faculty say about us: are there impressionistic measures we can use to see how well, or badly, we are working? What's life like outside the lecture room: are special events well-attended, like evening research seminars and occasional conferences? A Faculty is like a piece of hardware: it's an organisational device which aims to amplify all the virtues which higher education can offer for a sub-set of the university's community. The software is more complex: the people who work and study in it, and the ideas and knowledge, the skills and understanding they acquire and practise and test against accountable standards. Each summer, people leave the machine for other places, and the machine remains behind, albeit changed (subtly or significantly) by their process through it. Deans are the ones responsible for the nature of the machine, and for the quality of much of its software.

I sometimes look back to my time as an undergraduate (York, 1964-67). The people who ran 'new' universities in those days had a different task. It seems that Government said unto them: "Here's a green-field site close to a great and ancient city of much beauty, and here is some money. Go and build a university." (The famous story at the time was that the iconic water-tower at the University of York had been designed on the back of a beer mat by the Vice-Chancellor, Lord James of Rusholme, during a good night out, and lo! it came to be erected much as the sketch indicated.) That kind of higher education has gone, and some of the management skills needed to make it successful are less prominent now, while other, newer, ones have come to dominate. I wonder how Lord James and his colleagues would have managed things in the 1990s, the very point in my own career development where I happen to have reached a relatively senior position in this university. I like to think (I could be wrong) that they'd have foundered, that the constant battle against eroding resources and the need to be forever accountable would have been them off in their first term. Indeed, knowing then what we know today, I suspect that many of these energetic and inspiring people, burning with the excitement of their vision for university education in the 1960s, would never have allowed themselves to come within a mile of university management today. Too depressing!

But then again, the vision is not so different now, just different in scale. We're here to help people develop themselves as far as they can go, to become members of a community marked by knowledge and intellectual curiosity and confidence of action, leading for a few into the world of research, and for most into a useful, purposeful life in a complex modern democracy. We're giving our students a fuller and more precise set of tools for their lives. Just as universities did in the 1960s, but we're doing it for more people nowadays. Doing it in different ways. Doing it in a different society and for a more extensive range of purposes. Being a Dean here, difficult though it is (maintenance more than building), is nonetheless a privilege. The people are impressive, be they students or staff, and their purposes still have dignity. In some ways, they have an added seriousness, too, in comparison to that other higher education I look back to, because their successes are achieved against higher odds. So I'll go on professing that for a little while longer, assuming They let me.

A very peculiar practice: external examining in British universities

John Clayton

No professor in a British university can expect for long to escape being asked to serve as external examiner at undergraduate or postgraduate level at some other British university. Indeed, any professor who is not at least occasionally asked to act in this capacity should be concerned about their professional standing.

Employing external examiners is how British universities have traditionally tried to maintain academic standards in higher education and to ensure that students are treated fairly in the assessment of degree-level work from baccalaureate to doctorate. Never have these needs seemed greater than they do now, and never has the use of external examiners at undergraduate level been under more strain than it is at the moment.

Once upon a time, when Conservative ministers resigned on matters of honour and members of the Royal family did not get divorced and staff-student ratios were in single digits, British undergraduates were admitted to study a limited range of academic subjects with long-familiar names - like biology and physics, mathematics and economics, philosophy and classics. Having an honours degree meant that one had competence in the main branches of some academic discipline. Lecturers and professors could, with a little revision perhaps, teach or examine all branches of their discipline at least to honours level. In a few subjects, such as physics and philosophy, this is probably still the case. Honours degrees were assessed by written examinations taken typically in the last term of the final year of study. No matter where one did one's degree, the final examinations covered the main branches of the discipline, with scope for maybe one or at most two elective papers in areas of special interest to the student. Finals were in some ways comparable to American comprehensive exams. Anyone with a first or an upper-second was deemed by those who gave our state studentships and those who would supervise them to be sufficiently well equipped to undertake research for higher degrees.

In those happy times, it was easy enough to regard final examinations as measuring not just overall competence or level of attainment in a subject, but also as revealing a candidate's quality of mind. The degree result reflected a qualitative judgement by a board of examiners, who had shunned arithmetic and embraced instead a system of ciphers made up of letters (typically Greek) and every imaginable combination of plusses, queries and minuses. With all the subtlety that British academics are capable of mustering, examiners deliberated at what is for an American an alarmingly leisurely pace (approximating that of a cricket match) to decide if Smith's answers in Paper Two were nearer a β + ? + or a β + +.

For all the quirkiness of this very peculiar practice, however, something impressive was being transacted. A student's work was being assessed, not by formula-driven aggregation of marks given in separate courses by isolated tutors (in the manner of an American grade point average), but by the best collective judgment of a board of examiners based on qualities of mind exhibited overall in a set of examinations taken over three or four weeks and covering at least two years' effort by a student to become competent in a discipline and its main branches. Little wonder so much import could be attached to a degree classification, which an individual would carry, be it as a badge of honour or as an albatross, the rest of their life. And beyond. For their degree result would almost certainly find its way into their obituary as well: "Although X disappointed his tutors by just scraping a second, etc."

In this lost world of British academia, all the work on which the degree result would be based was on the table, so to say, and had been seen by several examiners, internal and external, all of them assessing work in areas of common expertise. There was also in this never-never land a consensus about the nature of a discipline and its main branches, so that (allowing for local variations at the borders) similar territory would be covered in final examinations wherever the discipline was taught. In such a world as this, it made sense for an external examiner to intervene in the discussion of borderline cases to say, "In my own University, Jenkins would be given a First," or whatever.

Having satisfied themselves that standards had been maintained and degree results fairly distributed, the examiners would go off to a festive dinner where they would overeat, overdrink and, as the mood slowly mellowed, exchange like measures of local and distant gossip, the most indiscreet stories circulating only with the port at the end of the feast. A more effective device for distributing gossip throughout British universities is difficult to imagine than the time-honoured ritual of transporting external examiners around the country in June each year.

Much of what has been recounted above survives in British universities today, not least the final feast and exchange of gossip, but the world of higher education idealised above exists only in collective memory and ritual re-enactment. At a time when more is being expected of external examiners than ever before by the CVCP and university administrators, the conditions under which the practice has to occur put the system of external examining under greater strain than it can long endure.

And this for at least three closely related reasons.

First, university expansion has accelerated in the past decade through fitful increases in student intake (without corresponding increases in the provision of academic staff) and, more recently, through absorption of former polytechnics into a formally unified but manifestly disparate system in which there is no longer any consensus about what constitutes a university or what counts as a proper subject of study or serves as the standard of assessment for an honours degree.

Second, Government-inflamed obsession with monitoring performance in higher education and CVCP-led insistence that universities are capable of self-regulation have placed additional weight on external examiners as the guarantors to students and their parents, their future employers and our paymasters that degree standards are being maintained and equitably applied, despite the rapid massification of British higher education. When I arrived in the UK in the late sixties, fewer than 10% of 18 year-olds went on to college or university; as late as 1979, no more than 12% entered higher education; by 1996, however, more than a third of 18 year-olds began a course in higher education.

Third, the fragmentation of learning through over-specialisation and the consolidation of interdisciplinary subject areas has made it unreasonable in many departments to expect any examiner, internal or external, to possess the expertise necessary to assess with confidence work done in all areas of the subject. It still remains common practice in small inter-disciplinary units for there to be no more than one external examiner, who is expected to monitor marking in all subjects covered, no matter how unfamiliar. In such cases, one person at least will have seen the full range of a student's work, even if much of it should be in territory beyond the external's acquaintance. In most cases, however, no one - not inside nor outside a department - will have seen all of any student's examinations, with the result that it is no longer possible for examiners to base judgements on their own assessment of a student's 'quality of mind' as encountered in the full range of examination work.

Increasingly, quantitative measurements have to be made; marks become numerical, not alphabetical. Much of the work that contributes to the assessment is no longer 'on the table' at examiners' meetings. Sometimes 40% or more of the degree awarded is based on coursework or 'cwa'. This is routinely seen by an external only if it constitutes 50% or more of the grade for any one unit. Some elements of assessment may be made up of examinations taken the previous year and the marks for these elements may already have been recorded. In some universities, such marks are fixed and cannot be altered even if an obviously rogue mark from the past should preclude the award of a higher class.

Given the circumstances that obtain in British higher education today, the future of external examining at under-graduate level must be in very serious doubt. The grounds traditionally offered in defence of this practice are remote from the reality encountered in British universities.

• The use of external examiners has not and, given the disparity of institutions and idiosyncrasy of assessment practices, cannot be expected to ensure uniformity of degree standards across the system. No one - not graduate admissions tutors nor funding councils nor personnel managers - imagines that a first-class honours degree from

the University of Southwest Central Rutland has the same standing as a first from a leading British research university.

- The use of external examiners has not been able to stem the upward drift of degree results in British universities. At one time, more students were awarded a 2:2 than any other degree; 2:1s were given for a strong performance and no more than 5% could expect a first or a third. Within the past decade, however, the 2:1 has become the norm. Fewer 2:2s than 2:1s are now routinely awarded, and thirds have become an endangered species. The number of firsts has increased sharply, with the result that a first no longer guarantees a studentship. Funding councils now ask referees to state if applicants received a weak (!), solid or outstanding first.

- Despite the best efforts of external examiners, their presence can no longer ensure either the absolute reliability or the relative fairness of internal marking. Sheer volume of work forces externals to limit attention to borderline scripts and does not allow them (as would have been expected at one time) independently to mark each script.

- The utter variety of degree regulations in force in different institutions has made it impossible to know what it would be for a similar standard to operate throughout the higher education system, much less to uphold that standard. It is a common enough experience for externals to watch a leaden 2:2 exam transform before their very eyes into a silver-plated 2:1 by the alchemy of high-grade coursework (invisible to the external's eyes) and the mumbled incantation of esoteric regulations of local provenance. Official regulations and private practices by boards at a few universities seem specifically designed to neutralise the effect of having an external examiner at all.

Whatever may be imagined to have happened in times of yore, external examiners today are forced to work under conditions that prevent their being able to do what is still expected of them. Comparability of academic standards across the system as a whole is a lost cause. *In the future as at present, in Britain as elsewhere, the value of an academic degree will continue to be backed by the good name of the institution that grants it.* Equability of marking within the individual units of each institution remains a legitimate concern, however. Blind double marking within a department, with an agreed system of adjudication, would seem sufficient to ensure fairness to individual students without prolonging the increasingly ineffective and vastly expensive practice of using external examiners after a decade and a half of ill-conceived expansion and chronic underfunding in British education.

Given the emotional attachment academics have to the system of external examining, however, the practice is likely to continue into the next millennium. And so long as the peculiar practice endures, professors will be in the front line of those expected to 'volunteer' to keep it afloat. Knowing as I do their dedication and sense of professional responsibility, British professors will continue to act as externals and will be unstinting in their efforts for the good of their students.

In small or very specialised fields, external examiners may be drawn from any rank, but when the numbers permit, there is a decided preference for more senior examiners. The Reynolds Report, which has become the law of the Medes and the Persians in these matters, stipulates that only persons of seniority and experience who are able to command authority should be appointed external examiners. Experience counts, of course, but one suspects that nervous university administrations prefer to use professors to give additional weight to their side if the institution is sued by a disgruntled student in an increasingly litigious society. It is in any case a duty which professors can scarcely avoid at some point in their careers; most professors will regularly be called upon to serve as examiners.

Some professors will be asked to serve as examiners at multiple institutions at once. The Reynolds Report recommends that no one should serve as an examiner for more than two institutions at the same time. With good reason, many institutions have built this requirement into their agreements with external examiners. In these days of inflated student numbers, however, it is far better to restrict oneself to taking on no more than *one* institution at a time. Not only does it keep one's marking load more manageable, it also makes it easier to arrange dates for examiners meetings in a crowded calendar and more difficult to confuse the sometimes complex and counter-intuitive examination regulations of one institution with those of another. I once marked one institution's scripts following a second institution's regulations. Not recommended for anyone with a sensitive nature; do it only if you have another post to go to in a distant country!

Partly because the system is overstretched, partly because of the frailty of human nature, things will go wrong from time to time. Do not be surprised *by anything* that occurs. Accept whatever befalls you with the courage and resignation of a Stoic/Calvinist/Buddhist (tick one) saint. Marks will be mis-recorded or misaveraged or misattributed - as when a 37 intended for 'Smith, R B' was given to 'Smith R', when the latter was hoping for a first and the former was going to be content with a pass degree. At one institution where I was examiner, an entire set of exam scripts went AWOL sometime between their being returned by the examiners and the examiners' meeting.

As an external you will encounter a degree of professionalism and good will that you never thought possible. You will also encounter instances of bloody-mindedness and meanness of spirit that you could not previously have imagined. At one university I arrived at my first examiners' meeting to find the staff of the section for which I was responsible so hostile and unyielding to one another that I was forced to assume the chairmanship of the meeting in order for us to make any headway at all. Part of the difficulty was deeply personal, but a large part of the problem was that the department in question had no shared view about what constituted a first or a 2:1 or a 2:2, etc. But guidelines are no use to those who will not be guided. At another institution, two internal markers were at such loggerheads that they refused to agree *any* marks. Sometimes there was a variance of only one percentage point between them, but they still could not agree whether a paper should be given 57 or 58 or even, to mention my hopelessly spineless suggestion, 57.5.

Unacceptable behaviour is not unknown among external examiners. I have known marks to be returned late (*mea culpa!*), thus creating difficulties for examinations officers who are required to prepare spreadsheets for use in the examiners' meeting or to report preliminary results to the registry. Such tardiness is discourteous and almost always without excuse. I have also known externals to lose concentration during examiners' meetings. On one amusing occasion I recall, we had been discussing for what seemed an eternity whether candidate 4417, an erratic but obviously bright enough student who had marks spread over the whole gamut, including (alas) more failures than are normally countenanced in an honours degree. The board did have discretion, however, to recommend that the candidate be given a third, rather than a pass. When asked his view, one external who had clearly had his mind elsewhere, looked hurriedly at the spread of marks, and upon seeing a few firsts but overlooking the failures, confidently said that the student would be given a first in his own university. I, for one, feared he might be right.

To any professor who is being asked for the first time to serve as an external, I conclude by offering nine suggestions borne of my experience as an examiner at universities, ancient and modern, civic and parkland, in England and Scotland.

First, do not agree to be an external examiner unless you are willing to do it properly - and know that this task will have to be given priority even when you have pressing responsibilities in your own department.

Second, know what is expected of you in each new appointment. If you think it is too little or too much, say so in writing at the outset. If unhappy with the conditions, make your position clear; and, if you get no joy, be willing to withdraw. You are entering into a professional contract, not involuntary servitude. It should not be assumed that external examiners have no say in the conditions of their service.

Third, read *all* the material that is sent to you at the beginning so that you know, eg the procedures and guidelines that operate locally. If you do not understand something or if a given practice seems eccentric or counter-intuitive, make enquiries. If, after seeing how the regulations work in practice, you still feel something is out of line, comment on it constructively in your annual report to the Vice-Chancellor.

Fourth, remember that you are there to maintain standards and ensure fairness to students, not to protect academics from embarrassment in cases of bloody-mindedness or professional malfeasance. Only if British universities can be seen to be capable of regulating themselves can they expect to convince Government that external regulation is unnecessary.

Fifth, read carefully all borderline scripts and enough of the remaining papers to satisfy yourself of the consistency of marking within and between units being examined. Where cwa is used to moderate exam results, insist that the department provide a spreadsheet showing the result for each student if the proposed examination results be allowed to stand. Also insist that any work used to make up the cwa mark be available for your inspection. Protest strongly if this is not done. If the department for which you are external examiner has no agreed statement of the attributes of a first, upper-second, lower-second, third, pass and fail script, insist that they produce one. Persist if they do not.

Sixth, assess draft examination papers carefully. Be sure that there is a good spread of questions, that they are concise and clear, that enough of them are 'open-ended' to allow better students a bit of scope, that the questions range widely enough to ensure that students have a reasonable choice consistent with the expectation that they demonstrate competence in the full range of the course, that the questions are fresh and not simply repeats from previous examinations.

Seventh, know who is responsible for what. Deal only with authorised persons in the department; do not deal directly with tutors of individual units unless requested to do so by the examinations officer. This helps minimise the chance of administrative confusion and the possibility of becoming innocently embroiled in internal difficulties. Make sure that fax lines or e-mail addresses are secure before using them to communicate sensitive information.

Eighth, make sure that the examinations officer provides as early in the year as possible dates when draft papers and examination scripts can be expected to arrive and the dates of the formal examiners' meeting. If your own university has a traditional three-term academic year and you are examining for a university on a semester system, be alert to the fact that their examinations are likely to occur twice a year.

Ninth, learn from the other institution: when you discover a practice or procedure that is better than what is used in your own department or university, commend it to your colleagues. By this means, good practice can be spread around the university system to the benefit of all. It is not only gossip that is effectively spread by external examining!

One of the Boys?

Johanna Laybourn-Parry

I frequently find myself in meetings with senior colleagues where I am the only woman, or sometimes one of a few women present. I am no longer conscious of being in the minority. I have spent all of my working life in that situation. It is simply that I am now part of an even smaller minority as a female professor. I am saddened by the fact that there are so few senior women staff in our universities, particularly in the sciences. The paucity of senior women is the result of a whole raft of contributory factors including lack of role models, the difficulty of combining a family life with an academic career, subtle and sometimes not so subtle discrimination and the disinclination of many women for power.

My first Chair was at La Trobe University in Melbourne, Australia. With hindsight I realise that the period I spent in Australia was extraordinarily valuable. It enabled me to crash through the glass ceiling and quickly acquire administrative and political experience I had hitherto lacked. Contrary to the British perceived image of a nation of beer swilling male chauvinist pigs who keep their Sheilas downtrodden, Australia has embraced the notion of equal opportunity wholeheartedly. It has strict laws which have achieved what equal opportunity legislation is designed to do; that is to change the way people think. The results are already clearly visible. There are a number of very senior women in science, and the science faculties in the universities have significant numbers of female professors and readers. It is easier for women to combine a family life with an academic career. Among the staff in the department I headed there were two women who had been appointed as half-time lecturers, so that they could rear their children. As part-timers they had both been promoted, one to a readership and the other to a senior lectureship. Working part-time in British academia effectively bars you from any hope of advancement. Most of my fellow female professors were or had been married, and had families. Obviously they did not have to sacrifice their personal lives on the altar of their careers as I have chosen to do. It would have been nice to have been able to enjoy both.

Australian law requires that all committees have gender balance of people with seniority appropriate to the remit of the committee. While such legislation does impose upon senior women, giving them a higher administrative load than their male colleagues, it ensures that they are thrown into the arena of university politics in a big way. After one has raced through a fast learning curve the advantages are considerable. One has the opportunity to change things and develop new ideas. I sat on some of the most important committees in the University. The small ones that make the decisions which are subsequently rubber stamped by the large committees. I also sat on a large number of Chair appointing committees, because all appointing committees must have women members of appropriate seniority. That was a very revealing experience. I was amazed by how badly some candidates for Chairs prepare their cases.

My male academic colleagues were tremendous. They treated me like one of the boys. If they went to the pub, I was always invited too. They were also gracious in their praise and support. For example, we were having difficulty recruiting students into the physical sciences, in common with all other universities in Australia. I realised that if the physical sciences floundered then the life sciences would suffer as a consequence. Something had to be done. My plan was to establish a degree in Environmental Science, essentially packaging physical sciences in another way. This had been mooted before, but had never got off the ground because the various departments concerned had always ended up squabbling about FTEs (full time student equivalents - or to put it crudely, dollars). I managed to get everyone working together, override the FTE issue so that altruism prevailed and launched a new degree. Much to my relief it attracted a good batch of students who had the highest entry scores in the Faculty. Both junior and senior colleagues congratulated and thanked me. A new experience for me, back in England I rarely received any praise for my efforts. When I got something wrong, however, a tonne of bricks landed rapidly on my head.

All was not perfect, however; there were vestiges of the old Aussie male to be found lurking in the crevices of academia. The technicians in the workshop of the Department I headed really did not like having a female boss. The retiring professor, who I replaced, had let the boys do much as they pleased, and they had certainly taken advantage of him. They were not happy with my new regime that demanded accountability and a full working week. The chief workshop technician, a somewhat surly individual, actually told me in no uncertain terms that he did not like having a woman boss. My response, couched with a charming smile and a sweet voice, was that it was entirely his problem; if I could tolerate his misogynism, he could learn to tolerate me. I also pointed out that he could resign anytime he wanted since I would have absolutely no difficulty replacing him. Thereafter I was known as the mother superior in the workshop and we lived with an uneasy truce, because they knew who held all the cards.

I was sorry to leave Australia, but family problems demanded that I return to the UK and I was lucky enough to be appointed to a Chair at Nottingham University. Australia had been an enjoyable two years but incredibly hard work, while I kept up my research, publishing rate, developed new teaching and carried a very large administrative load in both my department and the university. I had landed on my feet at Nottingham. It is an excellent university with undergraduates clamouring to enter its walls and a very high research profile. All the experience of participating in appointing other professors gave me a distinct advantage in the selection process for the chair I now hold at Nottingham. I was much amused when I found myself on a shortlist with a candidate I had interviewed for a chair in Australia a few weeks before. I knew exactly how I stood in relation to him.

I discovered that I was first female professor my Faculty had ever appointed. Like most UK universities, Nottingham has few female professors in the sciences. It took some of my fellow professors a little time to get used to having me in their ranks. There was a period when some of them preferred to hold a conversation with a point somewhere on my thorax, rather than my face. However, familiarity breeds contempt and I think they have quite got used to me now. I suspect the students found it quite a novelty. My freak value was high. I was told by one of my colleagues that one of her first year tutees had told her I was his kind of woman. I am uncertain as to whether this should be taken as a compliment.

Since returning to the UK I can see that we have some considerable way to go before we achieve the equity that Australia has. I dine out on the sexist remarks and wildly funny misunderstandings that arise because people do not expect to find a woman with the title of Professor. One may answer one's phone and be mistaken for the professor's secretary. Plumbers or electricians who come into my office to fix things remark that I do not look like a professor. "Oh really and what do professors look like?" I ask. The answers range from the obvious - "I did not expect a woman," to

"They are usually grey-haired old men." If one goes anywhere with a male colleague the assumption is that you are his underling, and all questions are addressed to him. Such occurrences were very much rarer in Australia.

It was not until I became a professor that I became fully aware of the responsibility I have as a role model for other women. When I got my first chair I was quite overwhelmed by the number of congratulatory cards and flowers I received from female colleagues and ex-students, who told me how much they admired me and what a great role model I was. It quite brought a lump to the throat. I really had no idea of the impact I was having on younger more junior women. Now I make a positive effort to encourage women students and colleagues. It is particularly important for female undergraduates and post-graduates to see what women can reach the higher echelons of the scientific profession. Somewhere between completing PhDs and climbing the career ladder they disappear.

I have realised that women lack an important ingredient for success. Quite simply they lack confidence. Most men do not suffer from that problem, or if they do, they hide it very successfully. I learned to be assertive and have confidence in myself many years ago. I was copying the men. I reasoned that if it worked for them it should work for me too. It has, I am now a professor but being assertive is not a characteristic which is considered attractive in a woman. I know I have been described as a pushy ambitious bitch. If I had been born a male, those attributes would not have been perceived as a failing. Such characteristics are seen as desirable in a male. At the same time I see no reason why a woman should sacrifice her femininity, even if some men are a trifle disconcerted by being confronted by a blue stocking who is not dressed in a tweed skirt and brogues with her hair squeezed into an untidy bun.

I am grateful for the experience that Australia gave me, because without it I know I would have found my new job at Nottingham very much more difficult. Leadership is a lonely experience, because you have effectively to cope with carrying the responsibility for your decisions without being able to discuss them with anyone in your department. You often have to make decisions which are not popular with all of your staff and sometimes you are unable, for reasons of confidentiality, to explain why you have made a particular decision. In Australia I was part of a social network of other more experienced professors with whom I could discuss issues. All the heads of Department in the Faculty met regularly for lunch and the heads of all the life sciences disciplines met regularly too. Having that facility was a great help. You discovered that problems you might be experiencing in managing your staff or budget were not unique to you. It was reassuring to discover that strategies you were adopting were similar to those adopted by others. One gained advice and support. I have not found it here, although I suspect that it exists among the men. Many years ago I remember reading about an eminent woman scientist in the University of London who expressed the same view. One does miss out on a good deal of the politics which one has to pick up by other means. It is not that there is a deliberate attempt to exclude women from the 'boy's club' it is simply that it does not occur to them to include you. Since I had the opportunity to serve my apprenticeship as a professor and head of department abroad, it has been much easier for me to cope without the support of a network here.

I sometimes wonder if I would follow the same career path if I had my time over again. If I had known twenty years ago what academia would evolve into and the sorry state of funding for science and education that this country now has, the answer would be most definitely not. Since one cannot foretell the future, I would probably have done it all over again despite the price I have paid for it. It has given me a great deal of fulfilment, and no other job would have taken me to the Antarctic to do research with my postdoctoral assistants and postgraduates. I still escape South at regular intervals, so I have a luxury that many other professors are denied, the chance to go back to being a simple field and laboratory scientist doing research uninterrupted by the phone and demands of running a department. Despite the fact that we have e-mail, phone and fax in Antarctica, it is less reliable than it is here, and consequently one can deny that things have reached you. You can always plead problems with the satellite link and ignore the outside world, at least for a brief divine period.

Professing a new discipline

Denis McCaldin

"Of course, our subject is a exception." How many times have academic colleagues heard a remark like this and quailed inwardly? But if we are to sustain and develop our chosen specialism we may well be obliged to engage in special pleading from time to time - even if our motives are misunderstood. Professing a new discipline demands many different levels of advocacy. The parameters of what constitutes an academic subject are always changing - and that is healthy. I hope that by using my particular experiences in the development of performance studies in music as a kind of case study, what I have to say here will strike a sympathetic chord with many colleagues working in other fields.

Music has a long history as an academic subject. Education in early Greek society was divided into two elements - Music and Gymnastic - and in *The Republic*, Plato delineated certain principles concerning the nature of music and education. These were subsequently recodified, most notably in a treatise by the Roman philosopher Boethius (ca 480-524 AD) entitled *De institutione musica*. His ideas proved very influential and by the later Middle Ages, the university curriculum was categorised into seven Liberal Arts. The Trivium formed the basis of the bachelor's degree and the Quadrivium, made up of Arithmetic, Astronomy, Geometry and Music, constituted the master's.

The world's first music degrees were conferred by Cambridge in 1463. Initially the awards seem to have been honorary, but by the beginning of the 16th century a compositional 'exercise' was a requirement. At Oxford a lectureship was founded in 1627 which involved taking weekly rehearsals.

This could imply that 'performance studies' were recognised early as part of the discipline; but in reality composition remained the most important element. For the next 250 years or so candidates for music degrees simply had to compose an 'exercise' and, only if it was approved, were they obliged to have it performed.

But even this modest performance requirement had disappeared by the end of the 19th century as the new conservatories of music, which were founded expressly to provide practical tuition, began to draw student performers away from universities. Soon there was an unhealthy divide between theory and practice. Although the decision to apportion the territory was never overtly articulated, increasingly the universities concentrated on critical matters and the conservatories on performance. In the 1920s and 30s, Cambridge partly anticipated the new subdiscipline of performance studies through its stage productions of Purcell and Handel operas. Here, very tentatively, the validity of offering performances informed by historical research began to be tested. It was an admirable beginning, but not powerful enough in itself to be taken seriously by other music faculties.

After World War Two, the nation's attitude to education changed. In universities, music courses were hastily devised to accommodate the large number of intending graduates and in the rush for validation, performance was largely ignored. But by the 1970s, the optimism generated by the Robbins report and the opportunity to invent different degree structures created fresh initiatives across the whole system. In truth, many of the new specialisms were not disciplines in the classic sense. Degree courses in economics, educational studies, politics, religion and sociology, which reflected modern culture soon began to proliferate. Soon other more traditional university subjects, like music, were caught up in the process of reassessing their relevance within the changing social order.

To be offered the opportunity to profess a new discipline, to start afresh and give impetus to experimentation within a traditional subject, was a chance not to be missed. It was a challenge to do something different. Creating diversity within the system could only be healthy. If mass education was going to benefit more of the population, then wider access should be by new pathways to a broader range of degree schemes.

For music, two external factors were particularly helpful. One was the burgeoning youth orchestra movement, the logical outcome of offering first class instrumental teaching nation-wide to children in primary and secondary schools. The standards attained in the best of these ensembles was astonishing. Those who became members of the National Youth Orchestra, for example, were trained by world class instrumentalists and performed in some of the most prestigious venues in the country. For many, their subsequent university experience was a let-down. The support was simply not there. They found that practical work was not always taken seriously, and that the staff who directed ensembles were rarely sufficiently trained themselves, often only undertaking such activities with reluctance. Furthermore, the course regulations prohibited even the most gifted individual players from offering performance as part of their degree assessment.

The other development was a growing fascination with so-called 'early music' - that is music composed before Bach and Handel. Finding little support at home, young university graduates like David Munrow and Christopher Hogwood travelled to specialist centres in Amsterdam or Vienna and returned full of enthusiasm. They began to explore the implications of historically informed performance practice in a more rigorous way than hitherto.

It was these two streams of influence, together with a dissatisfaction with existing degree schemes that first caused colleagues such as myself to suggest that a new discipline of 'performance studies in music' should be introduced as a matter of urgency. Our aim was to innovate - to illuminate and understand theory through practice. Establishing the subject and sustaining its credibility within the university system was to take time and effort.

In a 1975 review article on innovation in higher education, Alec Ross described four main features cited by a working party chaired by K G Collier[12] as the main criteria for establishing a new university discipline. They were the context, followed by the objectives, implementation and evaluation.

Context

The context of any new professorial initiative should perhaps ideally combine authority, unconventional thinking, and the codification of fresh initiatives. In the 1960s, established university departments already had an accepted core of sub-disciplines in music, but performance was not one of them. Research was based primarily on individual effort rather than teamwork and most academics were concerned with old music and scholarly criticism. Degree programmes reflected this. No credit was given for practical work and, although composition had been taught for generations, departments rarely felt obliged to stage professional performances as had been done

---

[12] see Alec Ross, review of K G Collier (ed), Innovation in Higher Education Series, *University Quarterly*, (Spring) 1975 pp 234-240.

in the time of Handel and Haydn. So, in professing the 'new' discipline of performance studies, we were in effect turning the clock back to the 18th century. This accords neatly with the cyclic view of history.

It was a lack of contact with the living experience of music and the absence of involvement with performers that provided the context for the creation of the new discipline of performance studies at university. The influence of youth orchestras and work on period instruments have already been mentioned but there was a further factor. Although it was abundantly clear that most of their students would never make careers as soloists, teaching at the music conservatoires was still geared to the creation of virtuosi. Bright school-leavers who were able to perform began looking for other options. Here then was the opportunity to offer them a new discipline within the university system; one rather less geared to vocational training than to the broader ideal of personal development. The aim was to synthesise the best elements from existing courses, which in this case spanned two different kinds of institution within higher education, by bridging the gap that had emerged between them over time. This approach fitted well with the philosophy of the '70s, when new universities were able to give entrepreneurial minds the chance to introduce more diversity into the system.

Objectives

The prime objective for any innovative discipline at university is to bring together like-minded intellects to explore perceived lacunae in existing knowledge. In the case of performance studies in music, the central idea was to explore theory through practice - a principle sometimes described as 'learning by doing' and one much developed since the '70s at all educational levels.

Implementation

Implementation of a new discipline is only possible with empowerment. In most cases, as well as a single-minded belief in the intrinsic worth of the embryonic subject there must be a desire to see it recognised both within the academy and beyond. Without a visionary vice-chancellor and understanding colleagues, the temptation to sideline any potential upstart (who may also become a rival) may stifle such a project at birth. The fortunate ones, myself included, faced serious debate about the merits and defects of our thinking. Research and teaching proposals were minutely scrutinised, and rightly so. But when defended, and colleagues' appropriate modifications included, it was usually given the senate's blessing. Most of the innovations were radical but not disruptive. In my case, elements of good practice found in other subjects and in other countries, along with personal research, were brought together to form the basis of the new discipline. Because our initiative was introduced at a time of relative affluence, like-minded staff were relatively easy to recruit, both from postgraduate schools and from among performers themselves. But there was a wariness too. Less sympathetic academics were reluctant to validate the work and in the early days peer group support, whether for research projects or for external examination, was sometimes hard to find. Furthermore, some conservatoire staff saw the universities' modest incursion into their sphere of influence as unhelpful and even impertinent.

Evaluation

Twenty years after inception may be an appropriate time to evaluate any new initiative and to ask how well it has succeeded. In many cases the spur towards innovation is a desire to improve accepted practice - to change something that *exists* for something that *should exist*. Whether the original concept remains more or less unaltered is one good indicator of its acceptance, as is its incorporation or rejection by the parent disciplines nearest to it.

Professing a new subject requires vision and enthusiasm, but it also requires good luck. Performance studies in music is an example of a recent initiative that has been fortunate. The initial courses were established in the 1970s, when morale within higher education was buoyant. From the beginning the subject received good support from students, both at undergraduate and postgraduate level. Today its relationship with other providers is healthy and respectful. In the competition for resources, the universities and conservatories have come much closer together and are united in their desire to defend their subject as robustly as they can. The discipline of performance studies is now a recognised part of degree studies in most British universities, but it is expensive - not least because it depends heavily on practical one-to-one tuition. Such a commitment, however central it may be to a new professorial subject, would not be countenanced so readily today. The opportunity was there twenty years ago, and some of us were able to take it. Although the present higher education system is less prosperous than it was before, the need for innovation and renewal does not change. If universities are to remain healthy, there must always be the opportunity and the resources for new minds to profess new disciplines.

Constructing Tension, Metastable Equilibrium or Downward Spiral?

Trevor Page

I have already seriously tried the patience of the remarkably tolerant Editor of this volume by being the last person to submit his contribution - late! However, as I view the increasing number of vertically-filed piles of recently-received 'active correspondence', 'please-review-thoroughly-and-respond-urgently research proposals and Journal submissions', quality-auditable teaching papers, my own research results (a decreasing pile) and various administrative chores (an increasing pile) around every available surface in my office, I realise that the very causes of my apparent tardiness are themselves the reasons for my current 'unease' in the Chair I hold. Of the two quotations pinned above my office door, one will serve well to introduce this article: approximately copied from an American colleague, it reads:

> "When you are up to your neck in alligators, it is difficult to remember that your original mission was to improve the locality by draining the swamp!"

Thus, while my Chair was established to provide 'leadership in teaching and research', my essential concern is that change - and, more specifically, the ever-increasing rate of change - in almost all areas of Academic life often make it difficult to judge which is the best direction to lead towards, let alone how quickly we should proceed along it for any advantageous outcome or optimised position for the future.

At the outset, I should explain that there are a number of aspects of Science and Engineering as university disciplines which differentiate them from Arts and Humanities though, as

I anticipate some of the growls of protest from my colleagues in other faculties, many of our underlying concerns are the same. However, these differences do serve to create significant additional pressures and tensions of their own and are worth at least touching on here.

One of the first of these pressures concerns the need to teach an ever-expanding curriculum which, somehow, must bridge the widening gap between 'where school subjects now finish' and the minimum threshold of the understanding of current science and engineering theories and practices commensurate with a degree programme (not to mention the expectations of a very wide spectrum of employers, many of whom increasingly expect degree programmes to be synonymous with 'vocational training'). Perhaps we should follow the advice of one of my senior industrial friends who pleads that we should concentrate on educating our students to take numerate, literate and 'soundly-based analytical approaches' to problem-solving, irrespective of the subject specialisms chosen as the framework to illustrate the principles of each course. Certainly we need to be more selective in choosing subject matter so as not to overload our courses. Looking back, it is clear that science students 'educated to analyse' in such ways were highly attractive to Banks, Finance Houses, and Investment Companies in the 70s and 80s and started the trend that science and engineering graduates did not always have to look for careers primarily in their subject areas. By contrast, I now see many industrial employers becoming less, rather than more, flexible in selecting candidates for employment and only offering their limited openings to applicants with some proven specialist knowledge (often determined by an on-the-spot exam) rather than those who may be more roundly educated and, in the longer term, more adaptable in their approaches. While four-year Masters courses may be an attractive solution to the problems of curriculum overload - and my colleagues and I have enjoyed rising to the challenges of designing several which we believe successful in both professional and educational terms - it is difficult to see how these sit comfortably with increased levels of student debt and diminishing resources for maintenance and sponsorship.

Further tensions are created by our subjects being laboratory-based, often with demands for expensive research equipment by which one's standing is all too often judged as if the very presence of the hardware, rather than the quality or originality of the work it enables, provides some measurable indicator of research 'virility'. Coupled with this, is the need to give our students essential practical experience in laboratories, where resources for equipment (again!) and manpower is constantly diminishing and under constant threat. Finally we have to submit to the demands of Professional Accreditation by bodies outside the University system who all too often demand some control over the structure and content of our courses without sharing the responsibility of having to either provide, or help us fight for, the enabling resources. While such challenges can provide tensions of a most constructive kind, for example in designing courses which are more efficient in terms of both time and resources than in the past, having to constantly modify courses to cope with year-by-year changes in circumstances is conducive neither to high quality teaching nor to good time management.

Now let me air three issues which, at first sight, ought to be bringing positive new challenges and initiatives to our subject, but which are often demanding further shifts in the delicate equilibrium of what we try to achieve. These are, wider access to higher education, public awareness of science, engineering and technology and the information technology revolution.

I am increasingly concerned about both the abilities and the changing expectations of some of our undergraduate students. While many of our students are as good as they ever were (no matter at what stage of their university careers their talents and enthusiasms fully develop), the national trend certainly seems to be for a smaller fraction of school leavers to be attracted into science and engineering but with a longer tail of lower abilities and motivation. I am unsure of the extent to which this is due to a perceived lack of exciting, well-paid careers in science, engineering and technology - and the adverts in the careers sections of national newspapers suggest that Industry could do far more to help UK Ltd in this area - and to what extent it is due to shortcomings in school curricula and teaching. Certainly there has to be something wrong in our education system when bright sixth formers complain of A-level physical science subjects being 'boring', 'dull' and 'over-demanding'. Compared to 20 years ago this same group now emerges with a higher level of factual knowledge but less systematic understanding of either basic principles or even the very rigours of definition and quantitative approaches upon which the subject areas rely. Thus, interviewees may claim to know all about the components of an aircraft engine (usually through a project) but have little idea of even the simplest principles upon which it works!! More fundamentally - and very explicitly because of over-reliance on calculators at too early a stage - few students now understand how to use mathematical functions such as logarithms and trigonometric functions and thus have great difficulties with log-log plots and other routine analytical methods. Telling them that, in the absence of pcs and calculators, the early US space programme relied greatly on slide rules and scientists/engineers who could make quick, sensible estimates by understanding the principles of calculations (and certainly without believing that their answers were always accurate to 10 significant digits!) usually results in looks of total disbelief!

Whether as a consequence of this, or as a symptom of the some other underlying problems such as increasing debts, I sense that the expectations of many undergraduates have also changed very markedly. "How do I approach this subject to really understand it?" has noticeably given way to "what is the minimum I need to do to pass?" While "are there any marks for it?" or "this is too hard - you want us to think!" or even "why are you telling me this if it is not going to be in the exam" are no longer apocryphal or even isolated responses to requests to read around the subject or attempt unassessed tutorial work. As a perceptive technician in my Department observed, "students now increasingly treat us as the supermarket of knowledge and browse the shelves taking as much or as little as they need to satisfy their short-term demands." However, when the demands of the various stages of in-course assessment are to be met, several UK and US universities are now experiencing a growth area in medical certificates quoting the newly-discovered and widely contagious affliction of 'performance anxiety' - interpreted as not expecting the students to be exposed to the pressures of submitting assessed work against previously-declared deadlines, not having to give oral presentations to their peer groups, and certainly not being interviewed by an External Examiner. In the days of teaching quality assessments, I believe that we need to explain that 'quality' makes demands that the taught - as well as their teachers - must be expected to fulfil from the outset.

It is a cause of both amusement and concern that, for the first time in my career, I have recently had the novel experiences of being asked (seriously) to stop a lecture while a student sharpened a pencil (apparently with the serious expectation that this was not an unreasonable request) and, reflecting the equality issues ever before us, being somewhat surprisingly accused (by a degree candidate) of being 'unfair' because, as

External Examiner, I had apparently (but quite inadvertently) interviewed the female student, who made the accusation, for a few minutes less than the male candidate who preceded her. Most clammy-handed candidates cannot wait for a viva to end, but apparently intent on making a point, this candidate had timed both interviews - but declined the offer of extending our discussions with some further questions. I was left unsure as to whether my assurances that she had dealt with my questions more quickly and effectively than her predecessor (true!) were accepted or not - but felt saddened and puzzled by her need to raise the issue at all.

With regard to my subject, it is a cause of great regret to me that somewhere we have failed to enthuse successive generations of youngsters, their parents, perhaps their teachers - and, certainly politicians - about the great challenges which have to be constantly met in trying to meet the demands of science, engineering and technology, not to mention the excitement and satisfaction to be experienced by successive generations of researchers and technologists in so doing! Indeed, the very quality of everyone's life depends on renewing the storehouses both of scholarship and of human resources trained to keep up the relentless technological demands of our everyday existence. Recently, I met with totally bemused looks when I explained to a large audience of sixth-formers that when Neil Armstrong set foot on the moon in 1969 (something they themselves volunteered as one of the apogees of twentieth century technology), he had not seen a PC, an electronic calculator, a CD player, a mobile phone, a jumbo jet, fibre-reinforced racing car bodies protecting their drivers in high speed crashes, family cars guaranteed against corrosion for longer than a year or even a crisp packet which would preserve the contents for years rather than weeks. Yet all these technological developments have been based on the 'appliance of science' and developed over a relatively short time-frame. Perhaps this lack of interest is not so surprising when the public expectations for ever-improving consumer goods are always high and the underlying science and technology is so well-disguised as to render them invisible to the vast majority. Generally, the ubiquitous 'man in the street' (interviewer for a local radio programme) usually believes that scientists and engineers contribute nothing to what he or she needs, or if they do, it has 'come from abroad'. This compares badly with levels of awareness in many parts of Europe and particularly Japan where tax increases to fund national science and technology programmes are usually welcomed as providing jobs and expanding the economy!

After two recent high profile international conferences, I realise that my primary worry about research centres is neither upon the increasing competition for decreasing 'pots' of research funding nor the volatile views of industrialists as to what role universities should be encouraged to play in the rich (but down-sizing) tapestry of national priorities and initiatives. Rather, it is the recent, but very noticeable, shortening of the 'half-life' of knowledge. Perhaps driven by the rapid rate at which information is being produced and accessed on the research front, few graduate researchers now have a significant awareness of any concept created more than 20 years ago. While this is currently far more pronounced in the USA, it is a trend that I cynically expect the UK to follow. More depressingly, this is also true of many more younger research supervisors let alone the management-oriented young bloods who are increasingly found to be the final arbiters of providing research contracts. As one of my US colleagues succinctly put it to me today, "If it is not on the Internet, then not only does it not exist - but it never even existed!" Thus I now hear conference presentations and have papers to referee - even more highly regarded schools - rediscovering what is already well known in other or older parts of the subject. My belief is that there are three reasons for this depressing trend. First, must be the intellectual (and physical) laziness which can so easily be the downside of electronic access to information. Second is the ephemeralism so easily induced by the needs to be seen to publish widely and be sure to be cited! Thus, many papers are now appearing which make copious references to the authors' own earlier work but no reference to either the background to the topic or those who developed the intellectual framework of which current is but a part. And yet for all this current activity, are there more good research papers around? I believe not. They are just more thinly spread over an ever increasing upwelling of journals - something which closes the circle by itself encouraging the fast 'on-line' search. Finally, I suspect that our own courses may also partly be to blame. By yielding to curriculum pressure and often teaching on a 'need-to-know' basis, perhaps we are guilty of distancing our students from a proper appreciation of basic concepts (though, often, these are not really changing that quickly). Thus, it may be significant that blocks of 1960s 'basic concepts' lectures are all too often précised and shoe-horned into small slots in current modules. Thus, perhaps a real long-term concern is whether or not we will recognise - and properly respond to - the dividing line between keeping course contents within manageable limits for our students and irretrievably 'dumbing' them down for future generations.

In attempting to respond to the challenge set by my Editor and distil my feelings of unease - rather than simply creating the 'usual whinge list' - I realise that 'time', or the lack of it, is the common factor to much of what I have written. Further, it is not simply a lack of quality thinking time, but more an increasing lack of 'rhythm' and 'structure' to the academic year. In particular, semesterisation has all too often resulted in many activities now seeming to be spread evenly and thinly. Thus, a well-defined 'examination' period (when all else was subordinate to the important problems of student assessment), has now become two or even three periods a year in which it is assumed that you are now available for endless other tasks because 'there is no teaching'! In my own case and with all universities increasingly moving the dates of their semesters, my own examining responsibilities, particularly with several universities now demanding two or three visits a year from their external examiners who have already made a detailed appraisal of at least two sets of examination papers, leaves almost no week in the October to June period free of setting, approving, moderating or otherwise being involved with examination papers and vivas. Further moves such as the removal of Research Council deadlines had led to funding submissions (and the consequent refereeing) being spread over the whole year with an interesting trend that the most frequent requests to referee project applications and final reports always come in the busiest examination periods. More papers, often submitted with a 'let's wait and see what the referee finds before we polish it into final form' attitude, only add to the load. Indeed, I sense that there are now many people both within and without the university system running with their agenda and independent schedules.

In conclusion, the factors which drew me to academic life have not changed. I continue to enjoy teaching, even though each year seems to bring an increased load, and still get a 'buzz' from seeing students who succeed in finally mastering new concepts. A student having difficulties suddenly lighting up with 'Eureka' in their eyes remains sheer satisfaction to a teacher. I also continue to get as great a level of satisfaction from research as I ever did, whether training and working with bright young researchers, discovering the elusive or having the floor at a major conference. But I really long for the time when I was *trusted* to do all these things to the best of my ability without constant assessments, checks and balances; when I did not have to fill in a form to justify taking an industrial sponsor to lunch; when 'blue skies' research was seen not only as important but was viewed as something which *might* pay something back in 20 years (rather than being scrapped if it was not commercially successful in two) and when 'please reply by return post' was a mark of sufficient urgency rather than 'I am waiting for your reply by return e-mail'.

However, I would also have to agree that many of the changes we have all experienced have had their good aspects. There is some truth in our now being leaner, fitter and more ready to respond to both changing needs and new initiatives. Many procedures emanating from both TQA and RAE exercises have brought higher standards and good practices to all and the IT revolution can be used, for example, to bring the benefits of computerised self-assessed teaching exercises to each and every student at his or her own pace. Thus, until the tensions I have described either exceed the strength of the system or stretch the tenacity and resourcefulness of its staff beyond breaking point, perhaps I will continue to hope that we may reverse the present tightening spiral and benefit from the positive aspects that continue enforced change may generate. The alternative down-slide is too nasty to contemplate.

As I finish editing this piece, my eyes turn to the second notice I now keep pinned over my door. Sent to me by a tongue-in-cheek administrator, and originating from another frustrated research colleague, it reads:

> "A Scholar's wisdom comes of ample leisure; if a man is to be wise he must be relieved of other tasks."
>
> [Ecclesiasticus 38. 24]

Perhaps this is the most telling commentary of all on the real cause of my unease!'

Other titles in the IHE Series:

They always eat green apples: *images of university and decisions at 16*
Mike Heathfield and Nina Wakeford
ISBN: 0 901800 16 3   Type: Paperback   Price: £6.95

Juggling for a degree: *mature students' experience of university life*
Edited by Hilary Arksey, Ian Marchant and Cheryl Simmill
ISBN: 0 901800 49 X   Type: Paperback   Price: £6.95

How's your dissertation going: *students share the rough reality of dissertation and project work*
Liz Hampson
ISBN: 0 901 800 51 1   Type: Paperback   Price: £6.95

In at the deep end: *first experiences of university teaching*
Edited by David Allan
ISBN: 0 901800 90 2   Type: Paperback   Price: £7.95

It's quite an education: *supporting your son or daughter through university*
Edited by Lynne Boundy
ISBN: 0 901800 98 8   Type: Paperback   Price: £7.95

Beg, borrow or starve?: *how to finance your degree*
Anthony Hesketh
ISBN: 0 901800 99 6   Type: Paperback   Price: £7.95

Take a Minute: *reflections on modern higher education administration*
Edited by Helena Thorley
ISBN: 1-86220-043-2   Type: Paperback   Price: £7.95

How to get a first class degree
New edition edited by Peter Tolmie
ISBN: 1-86220-044-0

48 Warm-ups for group work
Edited by Jo Malseed
Type: Spiral bound   Price: £4.95

For further information or to order any of the above titles please contact: Mrs Linda Cook, Unit for Innovation in Higher Education, Lonsdale College, Lancaster University, Lancaster LA1 4YN.
Tel: 01524 65201 ext 94522   Fax: 01524 843934
Email: l.cook@lancaster.ac.uk